OUT OF THE DEPTHS

*With backs to the wall, under the burden of weariness,
and in the gray light of futility, read Job and Jeremiah,
and hold on.*

Gottfried Benn

*The man who yearns for light must walk in darkness;
That which increases woe calls forth man's gladness.
True meaning reigns where all sense has departed;
Where no more ways exist there a new way has started.*

Manfred Hausmann

*Kept sweetly by a host of benign powers
We simply wait the future, come what may.
God is with us from morning till night's hours
And surely will be with us each new day.*

Dietrich Bonhoeffer

OUT
OF THE
DEPTHS

by Helmut Thielicke

Translated by G. W. BROMILEY

William B. Eerdmans Publishing Company
Grand Rapids, Michigan

The essays that appear here have been selected and translated from **Die Lebensangst** und ihre Ueberwindung *by special arrangements with the publisher, Gerd Mohn of Gütersloh, Germany.* © *C. Bertelsmann Verlag, Gütersloh 1954.*

Translator's Preface

The sermons, essays, and letters in this collection all date from the later war years and the immediate post-war years in Germany. Vivid pictures are given of what the defeat, collapse, and occupation meant for Christians and Christian pastors as they faced these events in faith and wrestled with their biblical interpretation. If there is little in the way of direct biblical exposition, the pieces give further evidence of the relevance, insight and power, and the ultimate biblical basis, of Thielicke's preaching and pastoral ministry. In so far as they deal with elemental and recurrent situations and issues, they still carry a living message for an apocalyptic age.

Pasadena, California, 1962

—G. W. BROMILEY

CONTENTS

1. *The God of Ends*

(*After an Air Raid*)

And as Jesus passed by, he saw a man which was blind from his birth.
And his disciples asked him, saying, Master, who did sin, this man, or his parents, that he was born blind?
Jesus answered, Neither hath this man sinned, nor his parents: but that the works of God should be made manifest in him (John 9:1-3).

A CHURCH as severely damaged as ours, standing in a waste of ruins, is the right place to read a passage such as this. We cannot, as usual, shut ourselves off for a short time behind the walls of our house of prayer and turn aside from all others to look only upon the Lord. We see mortally stricken houses through the gaping windows of our church. We cannot overlook the fact that horror is with us. The ruins themselves have a voice and a look in this hour. As Jesus says, the very stones cry out. What do they cry through these open windows? Are they making accusation, or are they perhaps raising a question, the dreadful question, "Why?"

There are many among us who have lost everything and who will find it hard to erase from their minds the horror they have suffered and the collapse of their individual world. And even if they do, they cannot blot out the specific question which we see whenever we look into their wounded and tortured eyes, the question, "Why?"

Many of our congregation who were perhaps with us last week are no longer engaging in the earthly worship of

9

God which we, wanderers and fugitives, celebrate. The tears have been wiped away from their eyes and they see with enlightened vision the enigmatic paths whose ends we cannot see, much as we should like to do so. When we consider these transfigured members of the congregation — and how can we help having them in our thoughts while questioning and seeking and yearning? — we note that they at least have a voice and a look, and that there is something they wish to say or indicate to us. What is it that the Church Triumphant has to say to the questioning ruins, to the questioning Church, and to the questioning world?

At root that which torments us most does not consist in difficult situations, in physical sorrows, or even in the great catastrophes which overtake our lives. When our soldiers came back in 1918, the national disaster was not the worst thing that awaited them. The worst thing was the question they brought back with them, the question, Why has so much blood been shed in vain? Why has all this had to come on Germany? They would perhaps have been more settled, and could perhaps have borne their burdens, if someone could have answered this question. Similarly, the men in our text are tormented by the question, How does it come about that the man born blind is stricken by the dreadful fate of everlasting night? What worries them is the question of suffering in the world, and especially of the strange and inexplicable distribution of suffering.

It is undoubtedly very remarkable that Jesus quite simply rejects this question. He did so on other occasions, for example, when He was asked why the tower which collapsed in Siloam fell on certain people and buried them in its ruins (Luke 13:1ff.). Why does Jesus not tackle these questions? Does He know nothing of what each of us knows or at least dimly suspects? Does He not accept the connection between guilt and punishment? In all misfortunes and catastrophes our deepest human instinct compels us to ask who the guilty ones are. We do so in this war. So terrible a disaster cannot have come by chance on the peoples of the West. It is not the playful whim of fate that millions are plunged into death and ancient cultures are obliterated. We feel that these are judgments. And where there is judgment, there is guilt. In all religions the priests bring sin offerings and the people join in penitential processions in times of war and terror, earthquake and fire. So deep is our sense of the underlying connection! And even when we cannot find a guilty party in some great or small misfortune, we invent one. So profound is our feeling on this point that behind sickness and death, behind bombs, ruined cities, and scattered families there has to be guilt. In face of all the horrors and woes of history and of our own lives, we have to raise the startling and insistent question, Why? An obscure feeling forces us to do so. It is the feeling and sense that we are now dealing with judgment and guilt.

We are again passing through one of the periods when we feel that we are very closely linked with the circle around Jesus. Their questions are ours; their hearts' torment is ours. We press close behind them, and we ask, and are all ears when Jesus answers. We are not alone before the Lord with our question — Why? To know even this is good and comforting.

What answer does Jesus give to the question concerning guilt, to the great question of our lives, the question of why. In the first place, His whole earthly life is an answer. When John sent the message from prison, "Art thou he that should come, or do we look for another?" Jesus sent back the reply: "Go and shew John again those things which ye do see and hear: the blind receive their sight, and the lame walk, the lepers are cleansed, and the deaf hear, the dead are raised up, and the poor have the gospel preached to them." Its meaning is that as Saviour He lays His gentle, healing hand on all the wounds of this world, both of body and of soul.

The wounds of the soul consist in a bad conscience and in the inner conflict of our hearts which are not right with

11

God and which have no peace. To these wounds of the
innermost man He says: "Thy sins are forgiven thee." The
other wounds of life are those inflicted by destiny and suffering, by sickness and poverty, by the violence of war, by
force, and by the sorrow of this world which constantly
makes us homeless within it. To this hurt of tormented
humanity Jesus says: "Rise, take up thy bed and walk."

Jesus knows and says quite a lot about the dreadful connection between guilt and suffering. He knows and says
that they are two sides to the alienation which man has
merited by breaking away from the Father. This is a world
that has torn itself free from the arms of the Father. It is
a cold world, in which one can be terribly alone. It is a
world in which one can perish without anyone knowing
about it. This world which has torn itself free from the
arms of the Father is a world in which there are mute graves
and sinister asylums, in which distrust and ambition raise their
Gorgon heads and the fiery red horseman of war inflames
the nations against one another.

There is a final, accusing guilt behind all these horrors, and
the waste of ruins around this church is a sign raised up by
God to show how far the destructive sorrow of a godless
world has already extended and to give us an inkling of how
monstrously it might yet increase.

In a terrifying vision Paul in Romans 8 sees even the mute
and unself-conscious creation plunged into great sighing
and groaning because it is implicated in the catastrophe which
man's separation from God has brought down. Often we
think that something of this is perceptible when we look into
the eyes of a dog.

I believe that today we are better able to understand and
to see, if we are not completely blinded, that all these things
are not owing to the blind march of fate, but that judgments
are being executed, that great visitations have begun, and
that the ruins and rubble, the smoke-filled sky and the new
graves are all calling us to repent, to make our peace with

God, to come back to the open arms of the Father from which we have broken away. For the doors of the Father's house are still open, and its light is still kindled.

But the text then raises a deeper question. For the disciples ask Jesus who has sinned, the man or his parents. They know all the things that we have just said. They have been brought up in the biblical tradition. They realize that there is a close connection between guilt and suffering. But a new question now arises. In this living encounter with a sick and tormented man, this new question is even more urgent and tormenting than the general question concerning guilt and suffering. I mean the question, Why has judgment fallen on *this* man? Why must he particularly suffer so much? Why did the tower of Siloam fall on the eighteen who were buried under it?

We might, of course, put the same question in the first person: Why must I go through my present suffering and face the ruin of my hopes? Did I not build up my home, which the bombs have shattered so dreadfully, with all the love of which I was capable? Did I not sacrifice myself for it? Did I not build into it all my good wishes for my aged parents or my children? Why was I struck? Or again, Why has my son or brother been snatched away? Was not his life full of hopes? What evil did he do? Did he not go forth with pure ideals? Who, then, has sinned, he or his parents? We cannot avoid this question. The great German tragedies (I am thinking not only of the *Nibelungenlied*) also have something to say concerning it.

Do we not all know this troublesome questioner within us who in contempt or despair, in sorrow or accusation constantly asks, "Why?" This little word "why" is no torrent of speech. It is only a little drop of three letters. Yet it can cause mortal injury to our souls.

The attitude of those who question Jesus is not that of inquisitive reporters who with ready pencils ask Him to say a few words on an interesting problem of life. For these men stand here in the name of the whole race, of all of us. And it is with burning eyes that they stand before Jesus and ask Him, Why this man? Why me?

Now we have already pointed to the remarkable fact that Jesus does not give any answer. Why is this? we ask again. Is His own soul wounded by this question? Has He nothing to say because He has a sudden vision of the cross on which He Himself will raise the question, Why? Why hast Thou forsaken Me, God?

No, it is not that He has nothing to say. He tells the people: Your question is wrongly put. Neither this man nor his parents sinned. God has a purpose for him. He is blind in order that the works of God should be manifested in him. And Jesus then heals him and visibly calls down the glory of God into this poor, dark life.

We go on to ask why Jesus rejects the question of why, and how we ought to ask, if this question is wrong. For we cannot simply stop asking and seeking. The darker it is around us, and the deeper the depths through which we must pass, the less can we do so.

First of all, then, we ask why Jesus rejects the question. So long as I ask *why* something happens to me, my thoughts are centered on self; and those whose ears are sharpened by the gospel detect also a measure of complaint — I have not deserved it. We constantly pretend that we know how God ought to act. This is reflected in the fact that we call Him "the dear Lord." But often, after years, or decades, we have to confess with shame how foolish and arrogant we were in complaining about the way in which He did act. How often have the dark hours in which we clenched our fists against heaven proved to be simply stations on the wise bypaths of His direction which we would not have missed for anything! Thus, by rejecting the question, Jesus helps to liberate us from constant complaint against God and from the injury which we do ourselves thereby.

14

Is this all that Jesus has to say on this pressing problem? Does He not also teach us to ask in a new way? He answers the questioners in our story as follows. The poor man is blind "in order that" the works of God may be revealed in him. He has thus been led into the night of blindness in order that the light of God's saving grace and wonderful direction may rise the more brightly about him. And indeed the miracle of healing in this story sheds a bright light on the whole night of suffering. It is part of the light which shines from the Saviour as He makes His way through the night of earth.

There is thus manifested a tremendous liberation, which Jesus brings to us in our need and in our bitter thoughts. For He teaches us to put our question in a way which is meaningful. He tells us that we should not ask "Why?" but "To what end?" In thus fashioning the question Jesus is a true Pastor. For when we understand the change, we are no longer choked with terror. We can breath again. We can cry and not be weary. We can live by the profound peace in our hearts.

Why is this such a tremendous liberation? When Jesus teaches us to ask to what end, we learn to look away from ourselves to God and to His future plans for our lives. We learn not to be immersed in our own thoughts. We are given a new, positive, and productive direction in our thinking.

Again and again it may be observed that sicknesses of spirit and incurable sorrows display the phenomena of what the physician calls an "egocentric structure." This means that in the darkest hours of this kind of melancholy our thoughts constantly revolve around ourselves: Why has this happened to me? What is to become of me? I see no way of escape. And the more I become immersed in myself, the more wretched I become. This wretchedness can lead to real sickness. All egocentric people are basically unhappy, for they want to be rulers of their own lives but with fatal certainty the moment is bound to come when they no longer know how.

But lo! Jesus now comes with stretched-out hand; He lifts up our heads and shows us how fortunate it is that we are not the rulers, but that God is in control, that He directs all things, and that He has a plan for us. So we suddenly look away from ourselves — and what an infinite blessing it is that we are no longer in the center of the picture, with that terrible sense of our own importance! We suddenly see the clouds, the air, the winds about us and realize that the One who directs their path and course will not forget me, that He has in view a goal for my way and wandering. This is the productive aspect of this new manner of questioning. We learn to look away from ourselves and to look to the ends which God has for our lives.

There is a second liberation. We men are dominated by the moment. If the sun shines, we rejoice to high heaven. If the bombs fall, everything seems to be lost. We can no longer see through the nearest cloud of dust. Our heart is defiant or despairing, and either way it is vacillating.

Jesus, however, frees us from the moment by His new question, To what end? He causes us to look to the future. God has something for you, and not for you alone, but for the whole world. God is a God of ends. Again and again the New Testament teaches us step by step to look to the end of all things when the confusing paths of our life, on which there are so many ruined hopes and graves of loved ones and neighbors, will reach their goal, and God's great thoughts of peace will be thought out to the end. The Revelation of John shows us how things will look at the ultimate end. Heaven will ring with the songs of praise of those who have overcome. They have all gone through the same tribulation as we have. They have suffered; they have been in distress in which they saw no heaven, no Father's eye; they have called out of the depths and cried, "Father, where art Thou?" But through it all they have sensed that

16

this "wrong" way through tears and vales of woe could only end thus in praise of God. Jesus causes us to see and hear this final praise when He teaches us to ask, To what end? This question gives me peace. For we cannot be nervous even in a dangerous situation if we know that it is going to end well, that it is all leading to a goal which is marked out for me and which means the very best for me. Christians are men who have a future to which they are conducted by a hand which is infinitely sure. They can lift up their heads because they know that this end is drawing near, however strange may be the way which leads to it, or which seems not to do so.

The third liberation which Jesus gives us through this question is perhaps the greatest. For when He asks to what end, He puts us to work and gives us a productive task. The best healing ointment for despair and depression is that of work, of tasks to perform.

To work through to the question of to what end, means work and discipline, an inner training. To turn aside from the negative question of why, means labor and effort. God is always positive. All that He does has a positive and helpful meaning. We have simply to be ready to go with Him on His way. Those who live in perpetual opposition can never see the purposes of God for them and they are always cutting across them. It is from such opposition that the Lord wills to free us when He teaches us the new form of the question. He thus gives our inward man a very clear working task. He has to fulfill it Himself, and He became our Forerunner in this fulfillment on the cross. Or do we imagine that it was no work for Him to work out and wrestle through the question: "My God, my God, why hast thou forsaken me?" to the final saying on the cross: "Father, into thy hands I commend my spirit," and therefore to final accord and peace with what the hands of God held for Him? It means work, a holy, inner discipline, not to look back to what God has taken from us but to look forward to the tasks which He is giving us.

I think of those wounded by bombs, of the bereaved and sorrowing, and I solemnly say to them, on the commission of Jesus and on the basis of our text, that with all their sorrow they are given a task.

Perhaps you are given the task to live for others more than you ever did when life was secure. Could you have really understood their needs if you had not yourself been plunged into these depths? Wounds must heal wounds. True helpers of their fellow men have always been those who were greatly hurt, who had to suffer great sorrows. Jesus could be our Pastor, our great High Priest, as the book of Hebrews calls Him, only because He Himself had to stand against the forces of guilt and suffering and death and thus He could have sympathy with those who sit in the shadow of these powers.

I ask, in the name of our text, Are you ready to go out and to seek the man who needs you, to find the task which God is giving you? I can only repeat with sacred monotony, God is always positive. He has something in view when He does something. He does it for a purpose. Do you see the field before you? It *is* a field; not the yawning waste of an uncertain future, as you supposed in your defiant despair. Put your hand to the plough, then, and do not look back.

It is very remarkable that Jesus calls the poor, that is, those who have lost everything, the lonely, the hungry, the thirsty, "blessed." Why does He do so? It is because He has something for them. Perhaps the ground has to give way under all of us, as under them, in order that we may ask where is the true ground on which we can build our lives. The very hour when all human security is shattered, when we are in the streets without either work or calling, when men turn from us, when our houses fall about us in ruins, when all is cold because our dearest friends are dead, when we are no longer able to see our way — this hour can be the most

18

blessed in our lives. For then God wills to be all things to us — home and friend, mother hand and food for the coming day, the place where we can lay our heads, the heart in which we can find rest and can be like the fowls of the air and the lilies of the field and say, "I have nothing, and now Thy hand must be all things to me."

Almost all fathers of our faith had to go through such testing fires. They had to live out as their own, in persecutions and afflictions, the destiny of the Master. They were often poorer than the foxes with their holes and the birds of the air with their nests. They were often hungrier than the lowliest beast. But when God did give them holes and nests and food, then they possessed these things as new men; they enjoyed them in a different way. They then learned to praise the dark hours when the coming day lay yet before them in dreadful obscurity and they did not yet know that only a thin partition separated them from the greatest surprises of God, so that instead of the coming day with its anxiety, eternity was granted to them.

It is to all these wonders which God has prepared that we should look, to surprises on the next stretch of the way, to tasks which He sets before us, to the many kindnesses which He will have waiting for us from the handclasp of a stranger to the laughter of a child. It is to these things that we should look, for these are the things God has in store for us and it is for this reason that Jesus teaches us to ask, To what end? God is a God of gifts and tasks.

Finally, we thus see that everything changes under our hands if with our hand in the hand of our Lord we are ready to march forward to the great ends of God. Our conscience is stained and we are guilty. But being in the hand of Jesus, we may ask with fear and trembling, "To what end?" and we may receive the answer of Paul: In order that grace may be mightier, the cross greater, and the Lord dearer to us.

Jesus, then, is the Redeemer of our heart and the One who transforms all things. He teaches us to look to the great ends of God because He Himself stands at this end. He is the One who will come again when the time is ripe. Everything is directed to this consummation of His work. There is sowing in tears during these years of terror, but the seed sown by God in good and pious hearts will ripen in the day of harvest. The hopeless confusion of nations and the destruction of proud traditions are the terrible signs of man who, alienated from God, is at the end of his own resources and is now asked whether he will let himself be summoned to a new beginning. The afflictions of your life and mine are the hollow ground under our feet which gives way because God wills to catch us.

All around us are ends and promises. The air is full of the divine question whether we are ready to come to Him and to accept the tasks He gives us. This is what Jesus means when He says that the darkness in the poor life of the man born blind, the darkness in your life and mine, is only to the end that the glory of God should be manifested thereby. This glory will come and it will be manifested in a most surprising way. It will come and be manifested in such a way as to astonish us, for God has a future for us, and He has not yet completed His plans.

Therefore, "Lift up your heads, for your redemption draweth nigh."

2. *On Death*

(Letter to a Soldier during the War)

YOU REMIND ME of the many prophecies before the war that if the apocalyptic horseman of war should again sweep over our country there would necessarily come a storm of inward awakening. From every possible illusion, idolatry, and web of empty words we would awaken again to the final true realities of death and God.

But now, while slowly convalescing after your hospitalization, you write that for most fellow soldiers this apparently plausible expectation has not been realized. Even truly apocalyptic encounters with death — with death in its most horrible forms and with a sadistic manifestation of human nature — have not proved to be, as expected, either a preaching of the Law or a visitation. Indeed, for the most part it seems that they have simply increased man's hardness. When we think that God's alarm clock must now surely stab every ear to attention, then the almost overpowering force of events seems to do the very opposite. Consciously or unconsciously, most people see in all this simply the revelation of naked struggle for power in which we must armor our souls with the proverbial "thick skin." "The play of forces and our related personal destinies are all in the hands of fate." That is usually the final conclusion.

Why is this so? You write concerning our fathers who fought in the first world war: "Even though their Christianity might have been dead, or conventional, or perverted by

21

Liberalism, they had at least learned a few hymns by heart, they knew a psalm or two, they knew some texts of Scripture which came to have a wonderful meaning in distress or danger or in the face of death. Thus the hidden seed sprang up after all when the sharp plough of war had broken up the hard soil. But is there a winter seed of this kind in our ground today? . . . Without this seed events remain inexplicable, and we best survive if we close our ears and trust in luck or fate." I believe that you have touched on the heart of the matter, even though this whole matter lies hidden in the hands of God and preserves its own secrets.

In the sacred history of the Old Testament we see that events as such — terrors, wars, natural disasters and popular awakenings — do not open up the way to God. Indeed, even the famous march of God through history did not command attention by its splendid display. Attention to God and union with Him came rather through the prophets and patriarchs who, by virtue of the divine Spirit with which they were invested, expounded this march and these events. The promise depends on the Word of God rather than on the march of God. It depends on the march only insofar as God must speak to distinguish it from the logical progress of events and from the apparent wonders which His human instruments perform as they stride with brazen steps across our planet. The moving of the mantle of God whose hem we would touch can leave men quite indifferent if God does not grant also the moving of His Spirit. If we do not see the same Lord behind both the poor garment of the Crucified and the rustling mantle of the second horseman of the Apocalypse, if we do not see Him in such a way as to perceive both these garments of eternal majesty, our eyes remain closed.

Thus I express my conviction that we should portray to men the poor garment of the Crucified only in such a way that we expound to them at the same time the rustling of the mantle of God in our age. God does not merely speak;

He also marches. And why should we not venture, why should we not have to venture, to speak of this marching when we have set ourselves under the discipline of His Word? Everything depends on whether we and our comrades live and move through all that God sends in the well-known light which He has given us for our feet. And perhaps theologians out of the pulpit, even more than preachers in it, are summoned today to hear the command of the hour and to become Socratic theologians, who will move through the markets and shelters and guard posts and command stations, and there, questioning and answering, often maintaining silence when others speak, from man to man, let this Word shine as a light in the darkness of events.

God's march through events cries out for those who will expound. For even the most stupid can see traces of something extraordinary. The point is that they do not know who it is that passes by. They do not know whether men make history, or history makes men, or fate, or the Lord of history.

One thing at least is clear, and with this you will agree. The imposing and dreadful things which we experience, especially death, put to us a question. Think only of the way in which we see ourselves constantly questioned by the manifestations of our mortality, especially in wartime. Think only of the New Year celebrations, when some stop their ears and cry out noisily, "Let us eat, drink and be merry, for tomorrow we die," while others approach this symbolic hour of mortality with prayer, setting it in the light of eternity. Think of both, and you will realize that all men in this moment hear the grass of time growing and all know that they are asked: On what way are you, and how far are you from its end? Men give different answers, but they are all asked. And I believe that we Socratic theologians, whom God has sent among our comrades, should tackle this question of death as it is raised by the New Year hour of war.

I will try to show you what I mean.

When the question of death cries out, many thrust wadding

into it and choke it, whether the cry comes through personal danger, or the death of a comrade, or by seeing the enemy lying in immobile ranks on the battle field. There are two such gags which we thrust into the jaws of screaming death.

The first is that death is part of nature. The rhythm of becoming and perishing is expressed in the necessity of dying. What more is there to it? It is still this rhythm even when the fury of war quickens its beat.

On this point let me tell you the following story. I am not interested in it for historical reasons, but because it is so relevant and has therefore such symbolical force at the present hour. A very gifted eighteen-year-old, a promising student, unknown to me, wrote to me about a publication of mine which had reached him. In his letter the storm and stress of the age of development was evident. He was well read, a genuine seeker, though his thoughts were perhaps ill-digested and exaggerated and speculative as is often the case with clever young people whose experience of life does not yet measure up to their mental endeavor. I pictured him as a lanky youth whose "inner organs" had hardly kept pace with the growth of his intellect. In my reply I shattered his structure of thought and advised him simply to do the truth towards his comrades in service and in danger. Only in this way, and not by abstract speculation, could he know whether "this teaching be of God." He wrote briefly to say that I was right, and that he would write again when he had worked and made progress along these lines, in prayer and action. He realized that he was only at the commencement. The next thing I received was the news of his death, and then I received part of a letter to me which had been found in his pack, telling of his first halting progress in this course. He fell before he was able to complete the letter.

Why am I telling you this? Because it came to me with overpowering force that here we do not find the rhythm of life. There is no such rhythm in the snatching away of this boy who stood only at the beginning. The rhythm here is rudely and drastically broken off in the middle of a letter. Can we not learn from this, cannot those whose experience is similar, learn that death is an enemy and a contradiction, that it ought not to be? Does it not come like a destroyer into the circles of life and friendship? Does it not take the best? Does it not make the lives of thousands but a fragment? Is it not truly unnatural and disorderly, as the Bible depicts it? I believe that much is already gained if we do not disguise this unnatural character by pathetic phrases. Even the greatness of a cause for which sacrifice is made must not blind us to the fact that something unique has to perish with all its promise, with all that God has designed for it.

Something unique! This leads us to the other gag that is used to silence the scream of death. For the truth is that one dies alone even though there is comradeship to give support until the final hour. We often sing the song:

> *Each alone, in narrow bed,*
> *Must join the ranks of the dead.*
> *Man finds that company bold and gay*
> *Falls away as the blossoms in May.*

Yet this is a lie. It may be a fact that lonely dying in a hospital bed reveals more clearly than dying on the field that death is like a barrier through which each must pass alone and over which is written: Your life is not transferrable; it belongs only to you, and with you it ends. I know, and I have experienced it myself as a soldier, that even in the midst of comradeship it is the individual whom death strikes. I thus see a marching company with rather different eyes. There is force in the march; the singing fuses the group into a single body — this is best appreciated when one is in the midst of it, and the marching and singing of comrades surround one on every hand, and private existence is extinguished. But I often think that each of those who march lives also in another dimension in which he cannot be represented, in which he is completely alone. Each bears his own guilt, his own anxiety, his own dying. I remember the end of a young soldier at whose death I had to be present in a hospital. Right at the last he said: "One dies here quite alone," even though his relatives were all gathered around him.

When we remember that death comes to us in this dimension, where we are alone, where everything falls away, where threads are snapped and cannot be tied again, then I believe that the masks, behind which the most profound messages of God for us are hidden, fall off.

When we recognize this, then we suddenly understand why death is taken so seriously in Holy Scripture. Nietzsche might think of it as the "future corruption" with whose help Christianity makes such "misuse of the hour of death." But we know better. The men of the Bible realized that we were called to a life in fellowship with God and that death is thus a physical disorder, that it is the last enemy. They realized that in the decisive things of life, in guilt, or the "mightiest hammer strokes of sorrow," man is alone and cannot be represented. They did not allow any illusions of collectivism to conceal the dimension in which my dying applies to me, in which I am alone before God, and in which, in spite of all the love and desire which cries out for eternity, for "deep, deep eternity," all living threads are snapped.

But I hear your counter-question: Should we then take serious things that seriously? Do not those who heroically despise death, who believe in fate, tread an easier path, which is perhaps the only one that most of us can tread, not looking into the depths but acting as we do at New Year?

You are right, dear friend. To despise death is easier. It is easier for the same reason a godless way is easier, because less restricted. Hence Luther contends against despisers, who could perhaps impress him at the human level, on the ground that they at the same time despise the One who permits death and that in blind defiance they spurn the message which death holds between its bony fingers, namely, the message

that here a boundary is marked out for the eternally bound-
less, that here a wall of separation is set up before the
eternity of God, a wall of separation which the rebel in us
will not accept and which we constantly try to tear down
in titanic revolt.

Nevertheless, I now put to you the question, What will
your comrades say if you evade the seriousness of the truth,
and specifically the seriousness of the truth of death, simply
because it is the truth? Is only that to be truth which serves
life? Does only that serve life which conceals its depths and
gives us the recklessness and unthinking productivity of
those who do not see dangers and who for this very reason
irresistibly overcome them?

Just recently I was talking with an eighteen-year-old soldier
who had been engaged in heavy fighting with the Russians.
We spoke of the way in which the Russians seemed to die
so easily, so enviably easily, so that often they would let
themselves be crushed by tanks rather than yield and would
still throw hand-grenades even when they themselves were
almost bloody pulp. Is that greatness, or heroism, or madness
— or what is it? With what seemed to me to be the sure instinct of youth the soldier explained it as follows. They die
so easily because they have nothing to lose. This is all there
is to it. For what do they lose when they lose themselves?
They do not know any Judge who sees them as individuals,
who will not let them be represented by others, who nails
them to themselves. They do not know the "infinite value
of the human soul" which is theirs as the soul of a creature,
of a child of God, of one who is dearly bought. What do
they lose, what do they believe they have to lose?

Dear friend, we are thus brought to the final mystery of
our faith. Death becomes the more serious the more we have
to lose, that is, the more we know the true destiny to which
we are called, the more we perceive the dignity and unique-
ness of our person to which death refers.

I know that in your case it is hardly necessary to issue

the warning that this dignity is not intrinsic to us as men and that it is not to be misunderstood along the lines of an empty individualism with its cult of personality. We can speak of the infinite value of the human soul only because we are infinitely loved and have been dearly bought. God does not love us because of our value; we have value because God loves us. It is because God's love rests upon us, because Jesus has died for us, that we have around our necks the golden chain, and upon our heads the crown, of which Luther speaks in the *Greater Catechism*. This crown makes us kingly, and not the other way around, as though we were given the crown because of our kingly figure. The Reformers spoke of the "alien righteousness" which we obtain through Jesus. In the same way we can speak of the "alien dignity" with which we are invested. This is the only true meaning of the infinite value of the human soul. And, mark well, it is quite against nature that we should have to die as such people. It is not an "it" that dies. It is not the body. It is not the individual in me. It is the person who is thus loved and who has this destiny. No one and nothing has ever thought or spoken so highly of man as the message of the Bible. For this reason, nowhere and in no writer do we find death treated with such seriousness, with such unmitigated and unrelieved gravity, as in the biblical message.

I cannot close this letter, however, without drawing your attention to a final insight. In such contexts Luther tells us that only He who inflicts and permits the wound of death can heal it. No other. Certainly not illusions of escapism. Even the Communist method of easy dying is no real healing. It teaches only a blind shedding of blood. It teaches only the ending of an anonymous collective magnitude. It does not teach the end of man who is taken out of his anonymity and who is "called by name." No, only God can heal the wound, because He inflicts it. Only He can heal whose love reveals to us so painfully, and yet with such blessing and promise, the infinite value of the human soul. For then we know that it is not an "it" which dies, but that *I* die; that the community which walks above my grave cannot represent me, but that I am truly and ineluctably and quite realistically at the end; and yet that I am one whose history with God cannot cease because I am thus called by name and because I am the companion of Jesus. I stand in the triumphant sphere of the power of the risen Lord, and it is again His alien life with which I have fellowship and which receives me on the far side of the dark grave. Not my quality of soul nor my supposed disposition for immortality will see me through, but this Pilgrim who marches at my side as my Lord and Brother and who can as little abandon me in the hereafter as let me fall from His hand on this side the grave.

You know the resurrection hymn of Paul Gerhardt:

> *I cling and cling forever,*
> *To Christ, my Lord and Head;*
> *There's nothing that can sever*
> *Us on the paths we tread.*
> *Yea though through death He go,*
> *Through world, through sin and woe,*
> *Though He may walk through hell,*
> *I'm His companion still.*

Ought we not to understand thus the march of God through the woes of history and the thousandfold death of battles? Must we not interpret and explain it in this way? May God give us the grace not to fail to pass on to our neighbors the message of this march!

3. Between the Horsemen of the Apocalypse
(1944)

> *And straightway he constrained his disciples to get into the ship, and to go to the other side before unto Bethsaida, while he sent away the people.*
>
> *And when he had sent them away, he departed into a mountain to pray.*
>
> *And when even was come, the ship was in the midst of the sea, and he alone on the land. And he saw them toiling in rowing; for the wind was contrary unto them; and about the fourth watch of the night he cometh unto them, walking upon the sea, and would have passed by them.*
>
> *But when they saw him walking upon the sea, they supposed it had been a spirit, and cried out:*
>
> *For they all saw him, and were troubled. And immediately he talked with them, and saith unto them, Be of good cheer; it is I; be not afraid.*
>
> *And he went up unto them into the ship, and the wind ceased: and they were sore amazed in themselves beyond measure, and wondered* (Mark 6:45-51).

OUR TEXT INTRODUCES us to two closely related worlds, both of which come upon us with power. Or should I say, two worlds which we ourselves experience?

On the one side there rages a fearful storm. The night rules with its apparitions and physical dangers. On that side is the world in which every man, the disciples as well as we, is filled up to the limit of endurance with the work and worry and conflict by which we can only try to insure the next hour and to protect to some degree our homes and our little ships. It is the world of burning, overtired eyes.

On the other side there predominates the stillness of Jesus' prayer. There all human clamor is hushed. Even the men who need His help fade from the scene — the people who under the burden of conscience and concern for the next day feel that they cannot last out any longer and who cry out so desperately and urgently for help. All must withdraw, for Jesus can be present with them only after He has first been with the Father. The Son of God Himself does not give out more in work and assistance than He has first received. For this reason He withdraws from men to take a few breaths of the air of eternity in prayer. Then He will be ready again for work, for the service of His brethren. Then He will be quite ready.

These two worlds, night and disaster on the one hand, and the stillness of prayer on the other, are here very close together. Are they not also very close together in us? Do we not all come out of unparalleled storms? Do we not still have in our eyes the tenacious and stubborn pictures of crashing beams, of the rain of scattering sparks and of racing fire engines? Do we not have in our ears the wail of sirens and the crack and collapse of homes about us? Are we not all a little overtired and exhausted from standing at our posts? Have we not all had to wrestle to get the hour of worship, stillness and listening? Would it not have been easier perhaps to spend this hour, too, in the rush and hurry of the last days and weeks, instead of stopping, instead of responding to the divine summons to halt, instead of allowing ourselves to be confronted with the question: Man, where art thou, where dost thou stand?

Certainly in this story of the storm and night of catastrophe on the one side, and the stillness of God for which we all thirst on the other, we have a depiction of the distress and longing of our own situation.

For all of us there thus arises necessarily this question: How do we stand in relation to the great stillness of Jesus amidst the unrest of men and the thousandfold distress which is about Him and about us all? How do we stand in relation to the great stillness of God within the volcanic crater in which we all live such exposed and dangerous lives?

After one of the most severe air attacks on any German city, a Christian who narrowly escaped death wrote to me, asking, "How come that I did not for a single moment think about God?"

This question, which we have perhaps put to ourselves already with a certain measure of pain and shock, does at least teach us that it is not self-evident that great disasters and anxieties should lead us to God. The Revelation of John reveals the strange and terrible fact that the visitations of God may often end by driving us into greater alienation and coldness, for it tells us that men did not repent when the woes and terrors of divine judgments broke upon them.

We note that our satanic opponent is always at work with inexhaustible ingenuity to set up a barrier between God and us. We normally think, of course, that fortune and comfort, wealth and joy in life constitute this partition, for we know that in times of sunshine and fortune we think we have no need of God. In such times we feel that we are full, and the cry for God, for the living God, is drowned by the brilliant symphony of life which causes us to enjoy to the full the intoxicating fact that we are alive:

> *Joy, thou fair Elysian daughter,*
> *Beauteous spark of deity,*
> *We approach with blissful rapture,*
> *Heavenly one, thy sanctuary.*

In such times man rejoices in his inner autarchy. He does not need any helping hand. He does not detect any flowing wound which must be bound up by God. He suppresses his guilt that cries out for forgiveness. The cross of Christ stands out above the stream of joy like a foreign body, like the bizarre *Mene tekel* of a dark world that has been conquered.

In these weeks of disaster, however, we have had a new experience. In these weeks of disaster we have seen that anxiety, fear of death, and feverish tension during nights of bombing can also be used by the devil to break our connection with God. This may come about simply through the fact that our days are so full of anxiety and waiting and the work of clearing and rescue that there is no place for other thoughts, and especially not for thoughts of God. Indeed, it may be noted further that even the ejaculatory prayers which we send up to heaven during the worst hours often fall back with broken wings from the reinforced cover of the shelter or the roof of the cellar.

Why is this? Very often in our anxious prayers we are not really speaking with God, but with the danger. We may make the following observation. I hear the whine of a bomb or the howl of a grenade. I perhaps break into the ejaculatory prayer, "Lord, help me!" but I am not really thinking of the Helper; I am thinking of the approaching missile.

Even in our prayers in danger, therefore, we note that we are rivetted to ourselves. The overpowering force of my cares or fears so confines me that I do not really seek the face of God. My prayer is simply the utterance of my inner stress. Thus in great terror I may be impelled to cry out, "O God!" just as an old man falling from a ladder may in his great fear scream out the primitive sound, "Mother!" But there is in these cases no real thought either of God or of one's mother, but only of a broken rung or of the impact of one's body on the ground.

There are people, perhaps ourselves included, who pray to God for specific things, for example, that their property may be preserved, or that they may pass an examination, or that someone dear to them may be kept alive. The thoughts of these people center on the thing they ask for. They are controlled by it. Their thoughts in prayer do not seek the face of God and therefore the face of the Lord who can give or deny what is asked for and who will either way display His love.

This sets before us one of the great dangers in prayer — a danger which can prevent us from attaining to true stillness in the storm and to the peace of heart of a genuine prayerful encounter with God. I mean the danger of clinging to ourselves, so that prayer is only an illusory chapel which we erect around the altar of our own desires and anxieties.

We must be careful to free ourselves from this great self-deception in prayer. We best win this freedom by noting the way in which Jesus converses with the Father in the stillness. We think especially of His high-priestly prayer in John 17. Here the Saviour speaks first of all and repeatedly words of praise and thanksgiving to the Father and of the fact that He will glorify His name. He thus seeks first the face of His Father; He seeks His glance; He touches His heart to hear its beat and to detect its love. He seeks the fatherly hand until He has it wholly in His own. Only then does He raise His own concerns. And even then He is not Himself the center of His prayer. His thoughts in prayer are for those entrusted to Him, for His disciples, for His people, for the countless multitude upon whom the darkness and gloom of an unredeemed world rest and who waste away in the shadow of death.

To pray in the name of Jesus is to follow in the footsteps of our praying Master. This means in practice that in the storms and fiery hurricanes of nights of bombing we shall not give rein to our natural instinct of self-preservation and simply dress it up a little in the gesture of prayer. For if we do, in spite of the pious words and the religious and liturgical formulation of this instinct and of our fears, we shall still be clinging to ourselves; and the hours in which we are only a breath from eternity will leave us unblessed and will remain in a twilight between horror and vacuity.

Instead, we must try to do the following two things: First, we must try truly to seek the hand of the Father and to rest in it. Amid all the whines and bursts and the shaking of our cellars we must say in prayer: "Whether we live or die, we are in Thy hand." This will help us through the fires and ruins, whether we see the sun rise again or whether it conducts us to the many dwellings of the Father, where our Lord and Saviour has prepared a place for us. The main thing is only and exclusively this hand in which we are hidden and the face of God in which His fatherly eye shines upon us. This eye, this hand, this heart, we must first seek.

Secondly, we must pray, not for ourselves alone, but for those around us, for the sick and helpless, for all who are not right with God and may be summoned to the throne of their Judge. We must pray for the houses of God in our city. We must commend the little children to God's angels.

We shall then learn with astonishment that in seeking God's hand and in priestly intercession for others we ourselves become calmer and wonderfully find the peace we sought in vain when we expressed our instinct of self-preservation in prayer.

Here, too, the rule is valid that if we seek first the kingdom of God, the face of God, the brethren, the laboring and heavy-laden, and all who are the apple of God's eye, then all other things, absolutely all other things, will be added unto us, including peace of heart and the knowledge of being upheld by the everlasting arms. When you pray for the anxious in your city, God will take away your anxiety. When you pray for the helpless, you will experience the help of God's mighty arm. When you pray for those who are not ready to be summoned before God's throne, you will experience the wonderful comfort of those who have a Saviour, a Saviour who will bring you through every judgment to the heart of the Father. These are the streams of living water which flow to us from the prayer of our Saviour.

A further thought strikes us as we contemplate the praying Christ. To discern it, let us consider the situation of the disciples. We are told that "when even was come, the ship was in the midst of the sea," and that they were "toiling in rowing."

"When even was come." We know what it means when the gray of night descends with the sinister things which it hides in its bosom, with its "terrors, specters, and fire hazards," of which our evening hymns speak — hymns which we could hardly understand in days of peace. We know what is meant by the kind of disaster by night which the disciples experience on the lake: the threatening noises whose cause we do not see; the overpowering force of the uncanny which is all about us; the sudden realization with unique alertness and clarity that the destiny of our ship, our house, our family depends on the initiative and energy which we display in the next minute, on the unrestrained courage with which we hazard our lives. Often there is not a second left for prayer. Particularly our brethren in uniform, who have constantly to live with these tensions, often tell us how their spiritual life withers and the very spirit of prayer threatens to die within them. Their tasks and inner tensions occupy them to such a degree that God can find no dwelling place in their souls.

But we should realize that there is One who constantly represents us by His prayer, even though we fail or are absent. Under the title "One Must Watch" Manfred Hausmann has given us a very helpful depiction of this based on the painting of Christ by Sigmaringen. Christ, with John on His breast, looks out upon the world with infinitely understanding and watchful eyes. He sees the afflictions and disasters of our tortured earth. He sees the people trembling in their cellars, the soldiers alone and uncared for dying on fields of battle. He sees the wordless and prayerless despair of the lonely whose life has ceased to have meaning. He sees all this with unparalleled clarity. No other man can bear this sight, and the eyes of Christ suggest the ultimate fullness of knowledge, of horror and of love. Therefore these eyes must remain open over it all: "One must watch."

In our text, too, we are told that while the disciples were fully occupied by what had to be done to meet the crisis, while they had no looks to spare for heaven and their lips were closed like a vice by their efforts, so that not even the slightest murmur of prayer could escape from them, then Jesus looks upon them and represents them with His prayer.

Perhaps the final thing which remains in times of inner dryness, wordless despair, and tumultuous impulse is that there is a place in the world where the link with the Father is not broken. This is the prayer of the One whom the New Testament calls our eternal High Priest. In the little ships of our lives we are so oppressed and harassed, so terribly empty of God and filled with anxiety, that we act as if we sensed nothing of His power. But it is a simple truth that One must watch, that One is in prayer for all. There is One who does not cease to lay our cold and unfeeling hands in the eternal hand of the Father. Christ stands on the mountain and prays while the disciples wrestle with death with closed mouths.

Many soldiers have told me, and I know from my own experience as a soldier, what a comfort it is in the midst of spiritual loneliness and weariness to know that somewhere at home there are praying congregations, that there are brothers and sisters who in my name maintain the link with God and engage in praise and thanksgiving and unceasing intercession. We are all gathered in the worship of God not only for our own edification but for this representative work which is taught us by our praying Saviour. There are needed ten men in the city who do not succumb to anxiety and horror under busy and unceasing activity, but who lift up their hands above the homes and the ruins, above the tasks and the enforced rest.

On this dark and tortured earth Heaven must see everywhere the points of light where two or three are gathered and do not let their hands fall. The world lives by virtue of this representative prayer of the community of Jesus, as the community itself lives by virtue of the prayer of the One who unceasingly watches over it.

This world lives by nothing else. It does not live by its technical discoveries. We have seen that the supposed progress of our century leads to chaos and consumes itself. Nor does it live by the frenzied dance of its little satisfactions. The song of joy breaks off suddenly when the shadow of death appears on the threshold. The world lives only by the prayer of the community of Jesus. It lives only by the prayer of the One who takes the last sigh of the anxious and dying and presents it to the throne of God. This prayer holds back judgments. It is because of this prayer that we still live.

Note should also be taken of two other points in our text. Jesus is not content merely to pray for His own. He also comes to them. He goes over the troubled sea and restrains its fury. Jesus is always with us in terror and disasters. Passion Week particularly teaches us how Jesus Himself enters the shadows of death to fetch us, and how He will not part from me even then when I must depart. Our text teaches us how Jesus Himself experiences all our isolations and temptations and anxieties and derelictions, that He may be like us, that He may be our Brother, and that He may have sympathy with us. Hence He is here in the storm and on the waves. He comes before the astonished eyes of His disciples as a radiant appearance.

And they — they regard Him as a ghost, as an illusion in the night of disaster. How is this?

We men are very strange. If the roaring of the hurricane and the tumult of the waves had suddenly ceased, and a sudden, gentle stillness had descended on turbulent nature, if roses had bloomed in the ruins, then we perhaps could believe that the Son of God had walked over the sea and the earth, as so often happens in fairy tales.

But that God should appear in the midst of the catastrophe never enters our heads. When the bombs spare one house and lay waste others, are we not all inclined to see the face of our heavenly Father turning into a mocking mask until it assumes the features of the sphinx of fate and accident? In the great sufferings through which we pass the reality of God threatens to turn into mere shadow. The world surely should have a more fatherly aspect if we are to believe in a Father. We simply cannot utter the words of the Psalmist: "Yea, though I walk through the valley of the shadow of death . . . thou art with me . . . ." God becomes a ghost, and Christ an illusion! Truly, we understand well enough what passed through the souls of the disciples at that time.

And yet this story shows quite plainly that God comes specifically and gladly into the midst of disasters and the sphere of death. If I were now to ask you when you had decisive encounters with God in your own lives, I should hardly be given the answer: "In hours of joy." Many would probably say: "I experienced such encounters when my world collapsed, when the great woes of history and of my own life broke over me." We are now beginning to sense why this is so. When the foundations of life totter, when our familiar home is surrounded by overwhelming sinister forces, and when we do not know whether we shall be victims or survivors in this apocalyptic conflict, it is then that we begin to examine afresh the foundations on which we can stand in time and eternity, and learn that we have here no abiding city. It is then that we realize one thing alone matters, namely, whether we have peace with God through Jesus Christ and are certain that neither death nor life can snatch us from the hand of God, from the hand which reaches for the leaking craft of our lives through the raging storm and in the name of which the Son comes to us.

Indeed, we men do not have the power, and are much too confused and too far from God, to produce this kind of divine view of life for ourselves and to make of everything temporal and terrible and destructive a parable. Of ourselves we only see the horror, and perhaps it is those people who take such unrestricted joy in life, the butterflies, who secretly and basically are most conscious of it, since otherwise they would not make such frenzied efforts to dance and flutter in the few rays of sunshine.

No, in order to see the fatherly hand of God behind the terror and the apocalyptic horsemen, one thing is needed, namely, that where we think we see a ghost or destiny, there we should hear a voice, saying, "Be of good cheer: it is I; be not afraid."

All praise and thanks be to God that we may hear this voice, "It is I." He Himself has said that He, and He alone, is the One who comes to us in terrors and judgments, that it is the fatherly hand which chastises us, and that it is the fatherly heart which brings us home. Listen to this voice in the present hour; listen to it even more so in the nights of bombing; listen to it in the moments when the dreaded letter comes; listen to it in the ruins of your homes; listen to it in the hours of hopelessness and despair. These things are not just the madness of men. They are not just a primitive eruption of our human misery. In and under the orgy of destruction to which God has delivered our race, there is another hand at work, the hand which seeks us, the hand which beckons to us and which with inconceivable fatherly goodness invites us to the table in the Father's house.

Therefore I bid you again to listen to this voice in all the tumult and destruction: "Be of good cheer; it is I; be not afraid." "Lo, I am with you alway, even unto the end of the world."

God be praised and thanked that this is not just a world of dreadful clamor but that there is also this voice, this one voice, which says: "It is I; be not afraid." "Why are ye fearful, O ye of little faith?"

4. *Theology in the Face of Death*

(*Letter to Friends on the Battlefield, November, 1944*)

WE HAVE SEEN Stuttgart burned and blasted, and we now know what is meant by the destruction of a "world." Only the language of the Bible is great enough to speak of the fire and smoke, of the wailing and gnashing of teeth, of endurance to the end and of love growing cold under the overpowering weight of affliction. Only the language of the Bible is powerful enough to speak of the unburied dead, of evil spirits in the air and of comforting angels. Only the Bible possesses the language for these things. This is why we have often failed to understand it. Our destiny has had too little specific gravity to initiate us deeply into the element of this language. But now that our own language is so inadequate in face of what we have experienced, we are beginning to sense the depths of this other language, even though for the most part we still do not understand it and in this dispensation never will.

This does not mean, of course, that men are more open to eternity because of what they have gone through. Affliction may teach us to pray, but it may also teach us to curse. We have no promise to the contrary. I often think of the clear-cut sayings in Revelation: in the terrors of the last time men did not repent. On the contrary, those to whom the terror of visitation applies, the ungodly, the secure, those who believe in fate, often feel their previous position confirmed, and they see cities and cultures perishing in flames simply as a symbol of the blind forces of destiny. It may be generally affirmed that in face of the overwhelming force of events, once the first shock has passed, men are not shaken out of their convictions. Excepting, perhaps, those whose views are not solidly based and who have thus no foundations to be shattered, men are for the most part confirmed in their opinions. The nihilist sees nothingness staring him in the face, and the Christian knows that the Father of Jesus Christ strides through the storms of fire in judgment and in grace. "For whosoever hath, to him shall be given; and whosoever hath not, from him shall be taken even that which he hath."

If, then, I try to evaluate these catastrophic events theologically, I certainly cannot speak of a revelation of God but only of a breaking up and making ready of the field, even though there is no certainty what seed will be sown in the furrows, whether the seed of demons or the seed of God.

We were returning from the Dodensee and heard on the way of the severe double attack on Stuttgart. When after tremendous tension and many detours and interruptions we finally reached the station at Bad Cannstatt, we asked an official whether we could get to our home in central Stuttgart. I shall never forget how he raised his hand toward heaven and said, "That is Stuttgart." There was a great pillar of smoke in the sky and the sun was obscured.

We had to walk from Cannstatt, making our way through a stream of refugees — old people, women, and children — who were all going the other way, their faces marked by horror, dirty and in the strangest assortment of clothing. One young woman trying to help her completely exhausted parents was wringing her hands in a mute and moving gesture of prayer. Perhaps worse than the disasters themselves is their reflection in the eyes of men. This reflection prepared us inwardly to such an extent that when we saw our burning house and even the glowing ruins of the Stiftskirche, we were not as much affected as we would otherwise have been.

Then followed days of feverish work to salvage our things, for part of our furniture had been moved into the street by soldiers. As soon as we sank into our beds at night, dead-tired, we were quickly roused by fresh warning, and then began a forced march to the shelters, where hundreds of people cramped themselves together in the Egyptian darkness underground. After some days we made the discovery that my wife's whole wardrobe and my gown had been stolen from the cellar.

One morning, when I was reflecting on this destruction of a whole world with all its tangible and intangible human, cultural and ecclesiastical aspects, and thinking also of the end of my own work in Stuttgart, I suddenly found myself before a great crater caused by a heavy bomb which had plunged through the reinforced roof of a cellar. More than fifty young men had found a terrible death in this hole. A woman approached me and asked my name, since she was not sure who I was in my rather Bohemian attire. She said, "My husband was killed here. The rescue party did not find a trace of him. Last Thursday evening he went with me to your church. And here before this cavity I want to thank you for helping to prepare him for eternity." Thus God is able to comfort; thus He is able suddenly and abruptly and mercifully to transform a person.

The brief but difficult time of homelessness which followed reminded me above all how much status we lose in human eyes — which do not look upon the heart — when we no longer appear to have anything, and how very few of those who have possessions, or who live outside the disaster areas, are in a position to understand this state of absolute poverty, let alone to place themselves in the mood of refugees or of those who have suffered harm or loss. There is here a terrible and constricting loneliness which on the human level finds little comfort in the great number of fellow sufferers, since the totalness of the disaster involves preoccupation with oneself and one's own ruins. The earlier, partial attacks, which had been heavy enough, came to appear almost "idyllic" from this standpoint.

I rearranged my lectures at Cannstatt, and how venture-some were our expeditions there, how comfortless for most of us the nightly return through heaps of rubble where there was no cover, how unending the many stretches where there were no streets! Yet a good company assembled which could hardly be squeezed into the Luther Hall. Then another heavy double raid blasted us out of this building, too, so that I could speak only in Ludwigsburg, since there was not a single church left in the whole city of Stuttgart.

During the concluding prayer one night the siren blew an alert. The hall was packed, and so it emptied very slowly. I was one of the last to leave, and in the heavy anti-aircraft fire I found it hard to see my way to the shelter because the night was dark. I was pulled in together with a young friend just as the first explosions began. Our return was most adventurous. We had to go through a herd of startled cows, past the barbed-wire fences of prisoner-of-war camps, and then through burning streets. We had hardly arrived back before a new and heavy attack broke loose. Two people who had been present at the meeting were killed on the way home, including the organist, who shortly before had played the evening hymn "Mein schönste Zier."

As I now work at the transcript of my series of lectures, I am under the deep impression that they were all pro-jected and delivered as a "theology in the face of death." It will perhaps become obvious later how heavily burdened and perhaps also blessed they were with the accent of utmost seriousness. In them there was no room for secondary things; they always plunged the audience into the uncertainty of the sphere of death, and each theological thought, there-fore, was forced to steer clear from the speculative and to unlock the ultimate content of evangelical comfort. So I cherish the hope that these words spoken in broken pulpits and under shattered spires, whose hearers are now scattered to the winds and to every kind of homelessness, have gained rather than lost by the proximity of death and the nearness of eternity. Therefore I want them to maintain their relevance to the time of delivery, since this time was and is linked with eternity in a way both threatening and yet also comforting, and since it thus corrects rather than distorts our insight into the proportions of what is truly great and what is truly small.

It is thus with comfort that we pass into the uncertain future, into the coming weeks and moments in which one thing alone can be fully certain, namely, that we are to commemorate the advent of the Lord, that He comes and comes with power and is ever drawing nearer. Today perhaps more than ever before we men must let our broodings and desires and anxieties be taken up into the gracious hands of God. We have indeed a Lord who can go through prison walls, through barbed wire and across the sea, who laughs at His human opponents. We must all be conscious of this defiant and confident laughing of Christ, which in the hymn of J. Franck, "Jesu, meine Freude" ("Jesus My Joy"), echoes from the fragile walls of this world and goes forth from the sheltering wind-breaks of its great storms. We can be calm because we know one thing for sure, come what may: the tokens of God's grace will always be greater than our tribulation.

We must all experience this theology in the face of death. We have lingered too long in the shelter of the abstract. All the great experiences of the Church have ripened in the threatening proximity of death.

In the New Testament, too, there is reference to uplifted heads and therefore to those who do not shelter themselves from the bombardment of events but who hold their heads high because they hear Someone coming from the other side. They suddenly realize that those who shoot so hard are themselves caught up in a strategic conception of which they have no inkling, and that the One who comes, and towards whom our heads are uplifted, regards them all as fools. What men plan for evil God is able to overrule for good. The cunning devices of the devil become an act in salvation history — no less! Everything, literally everything, happens very differently from what we imagine. Everything, literally everything, happens exactly as we dare to hope in those moments when we show the greatest abandon in our faith in Jesus Christ.

5. *In the Depths*

*(Letter to a Young Girl in the Early Days
of the Occupation, 1945)*

I UNDERSTAND SO WELL the things you write about. I was in
D. during the worst days and I heard there that in a neigh-
boring village in which there was no pastor and no one else
in authority the women had suffered terrible things. So
I went there at once and visited all those of whom I
had heard. In the evening the women, filled with unreason-
ing anxiety, gathered in the church and school, and slept
with their children on straw mattresses. I held evening
prayers with them, and I have never entered the pulpit so
gladly or in such strange circumstances. I told them how the
infant Christ lay on hay and straw and that it was only thus
that the church itself was consecrated. He who bore our
human shame from the very day of His birth was now among
them, among those who had been shamed. If they were open
to Him, they could experience His presence better than in
hours of supreme spiritual loftiness. The greatest moments
of my own life have always been in similar circumstances
and not in times spent in theology or in my academic office,
which I love very much and in which God can bless me
richly too.

I find painful joy in your unqualified honesty. You say
that you will not praise God at all if you have to do it out
of hypocrisy. You can take no comfort in the thought that
even this terrible event passed before the eyes of God and

was censored by Him before it affected you. You will not pretend to believe what you cannot really believe, namely, that this dreadful experience must have been for the best for you.

Do not think that I am now going to try to answer the question which burdens you. I, too, am familiar with insoluble riddles which torture me. Besides, I have too much respect for your grief and earnestness to afflict you with speculations. But perhaps I may say a few things more on the question you raise in your letter — whether all this worked out for the best. Perhaps God does not even want us to raise this question. Perhaps that is one of the last things we shall be able to admit, that the worst things worked out for the best. Perhaps we shall be able to say this only at the Day of Judgment, whereas while we are here below we can only believe it. Therefore for the present we must not ask in relation to ourselves, not even in relation to our own piety and our soul's salvation.

It could indeed very well be that God purposefully includes His people in the judgments that have fallen and are falling on our whole nation, and that in that most dreadful moment of your life He has thus wrapped you up in the guilt of our nation, so that He calls to you: "I have heard it! And believe Me, what you prayed then is never lost. No single word that a desperate and trusting soul cries out to Me will be lost in My eternity. And you will one day be astonished how differently and how wonderfully your prayer was answered. But exactly because you are a graciously favored one, simply because you know Me and may believe in Me, I did not wish to preserve you from the shame of your people, and to spare you My judgments and set you apart. My righteous people must be present where My judgments are. They must be there in My visitations. Or have you no part in the guilt which has provoked all these judgments? Because you do not have such a dramatic share in the special sins of the age, may you claim special treatment? Should I spare the houses and bodies of My own? Should I not rather risk the danger that their love may grow cold in the midst of judgments than the much greater danger that in their public preservation they will lose their love for their guilty brothers and sisters who are brought under judgment, and that they finally will proudly say: 'I am not as they are . . .'? What do you think, then, that it means to Me, this thing that causes the praise of the heavenly choirs to soar when a pure girl as terribly shamed as you have been, learns to accept it for the sake of her guilty and impure brothers and sisters, when she is quite simply prepared to stand by them in their very real shame, when she will not hold aloof from them in spite of her pure body and undefiled soul, when she learns to say under all this: 'My fault, my own most grievous fault!'? Do you not believe that streams of living water can flow from a body thus defiled and that this experience of suffering surely will bear unheard of fruit in My kingdom?"

How would it be if you were to ask along these lines and God would give you some such answer? I certainly believe that if you could learn to understand your grief in relation to the total guilt, if you could thus be awakened to a wholly new understanding and a wholly new consolation, and if in your future life you could point out to the tormented and guilty that you yourself had had to suffer this incomparable injury, then one day you would be able to see this terrible night as something which is laden with the fullness of hidden blessing (even though now you are as little able to do this as I am), so that ultimately, having first been for the good of others, it will turn out to have been for the best for you too.

With this heavy burden God has given you a task, and everything now depends on what you do with it. He has certainly not given it to you for brooding about it. Nor has He done so to disturb your imagination. I know that we cannot simply repress our imagination. The will is of little use at this point. But when these terrifying pictures arise, think of that other body that was shamed because He accepted solidarity with a guilt and with judgments in the midst of which He was as little in place as a pure virgin in a brothel. And if you cannot avoid the impression of the silence of God and your own helplessness and forsakenness in that hour, do not strain your will but think of the helpless forsakenness of that lonely figure on the cross who cried: "My God, my God, why hast thou forsaken me?" You and I, of course, have every reason to be abandoned by God, for how often do we not abandon Him! But this One never abandoned God; yet He had so great a love that He let Himself be abandoned along with His brothers when they plunged into guilty forsakenness.

This hour, too, will surely look quite different when seen from the standpoint of the hereafter at the Last Day. It will become "that moment" — no more! — that moment when we were forsaken and after which He gathered us to Himself with greater mercies (Isa. 54:7). We must all be plunged into the depths, from which we then shall cry, because it is only there that God can come to us with the fullness of His blessing.

I should also like to say this: I hope that some day you will find definite help in real love for a man. What you have experienced has nothing, absolutely nothing whatever, to do with what I desire that you may some day experience in all its fullness. Perhaps then none better can evaluate than you the richness of what God has given to the body, since few have experienced as you have the way in which this greatest of gifts can be desecrated and can fall among thieves. Your life is truly full of tasks, of rewarding tasks.

6. *The Question Concerning the Gracious God*

IT IS HARD TO THINK of Luther's question, "How can I find a gracious God?", as being uttered by a contemporary voice or written in a modern work. It seems to have about it something of the atmosphere — respectable, no doubt — of the pig-leather girdle and the monastery cell, but not of the air which our own age breathes, the air of the stadium or the smog of the big city.

If we were to try to find a modern equivalent it would probably be the question: "Where is God?" In this question we all feel that we are understood. It involves no alien or dead terms. We can hear it in films and novels. It may be asked in cafés; for it can be asked without pathos or a preaching voice. It can be raised just as naturally as all other serious things are usually discussed by serious men.

Why do we formulate this question so easily? One reason is that it is so entirely our own question. It expresses our inner self. This is surely no small part of its attraction. The following consideration will perhaps help us. Many people today hesitate to go to a pastor because they think that he will simply apply to their problem some ready-made dogmatic formula in which he does not express himself (as they are doing) and which he does not basically share. They thus prefer to go to other men and women whom they meet in the office or on the train or in the street. It is not that these people can give them a patent remedy for the problem which bothers them. The only answer they want is a little sympathy and understanding. They do not want an answer in

51

the strict sense. They certainly do not want anything ready-made and therefore alien. What we require in all the various needs and problems of our age is a sympathetic person who is perhaps as perplexed and troubled as we are, not the consolation of a peace which is above and beyond the question and which can be had only as it is proclaimed. What we desire is not a voice from beyond, but a voice which comes from this world, the voice of brother men in solidarity with us, the voice which chimes in with the chorus of the struggling and oppressed.

It is for this reason that we find this question a natural one. It expresses everything that disturbs us. In it rings the implied question concerning the meaning of puzzling and terrible events and higher thoughts and higher ways. It expresses the plain, oppressive and compelling distress caused by such events. Perhaps it also echoes only silence, a silence which we do not expect to be broken and in which the unanswered question evaporates. Sometimes the question "Where is God?" is understood rhetorically. It is an open and recurrent question, like that of Pilate concerning truth. Whoever puts it simply as a question betrays a solidarity of unease and oppression with the one of whom it is asked. He simply gives voice to that which disturbs me too. And already this gives a measure of comfort and pastoral help, even though the question is never answered and certainly not dogmatically so.

We feel so understood in this question, "Where is God?" and find it so attractive for the very reason that it remains open and pressing. In their more relaxed moments the most serious pagans of our day all have this type of question in their eyes and many even on their lips.

Now it is a remarkable fact that although there is a sense of distress in Luther's question too, it has a very different character. It does not ring out as a question, nor does man express himself in it. He does not wait for the chorus of his fellow men to chime in with it. No, strange though it may sound, Luther's question is not a monologue of man but the answer in a dialogue. The first word in this dialogue was God's question, the question, "Adam — man — where art thou?" This was the question of judgment; it is the question by which we are arrested and must suddenly stand still and look God in the eyes.

In this moment when I must stand still I suddenly know what I did not know or even remotely suspect before — that it is not a pleasant thing, but something very dreadful, to have to stand still and to answer God. For, strictly speaking, it is not that I *may* stand still and speak with God: I *must* do so. And that is dreadful because of all the things that I would like to conceal and hold behind my back, lest God should see them. But this God views me so strangely that it seems as if my body is transparent like glass and He sees the hand behind my back *with* the secret things in it and *without* the things He laid in it which I have lost.

Naturally, I, Adam, am afraid. This is not just because I can see no escape from the dialogue; but most of all because of the surprise. I never thought it possible that God could thus meet me in the way. I regarded it as a product of anthropomorphic fancy that He could have angry eyes. I found the question concerning God interesting, and believed it made me interesting too. How could I suspect that after the electric question concerning God, the answer of God should carry this mortal voltage? (That this is so may be seen quite simply from the fact that in this answer of God it is not a matter of my answer to God's question but of God's own answer, of the summons which brings me to a halt: "Here am I!")

The first moment I am thus forced — at long last forced — to take God seriously, and not merely to speak, to question, and to dispute concerning Him, this first moment of seriousness shows me that I am not in a relationship of friend with God. He is not God my Friend, simply because I am not man His friend. Why else should I hold my hand behind my back, the hand with the many things that are in it and without the many things that should be in it, the hand which is therefore a fist clenched against God because it encloses so many things it cannot let go!

Hence there now arises the second word in the dialogue, the word concerning the gracious God, which, though put in the form of a question, is really an answer. We cannot understand this if we do not remember the opening of the dialogue. Only the flighty and immature curiously begin a novel at the end. But we are by and large flighty today, and we act as if God's dealings were a bad novel which can be begun at the end. We secularized interpreters of Christianity begin our criticism with the stammerings of man rather than with Him who gave us the strength to stammer, and in so doing we imagine that man cannot solve the problem concerning himself — none but we, of course! — and meanwhile we cannot truly solve the problem concerning God.

In a monologue or in terms of self-expression the question "How can I find a gracious God?" is merely religious psychopathy. But when we see that there is another figure on the other side of the table, and that the question is only part of a conversation preceded and followed by many other things, then it is deadly serious.

If we are really to get the sense of Luther's question, we must free ourselves completely from the notion that what we have is simply a particularly intensive religious experience which in intuitive realism and a brilliant sense of religious reality goes beyond the normal question "Where is God?" No, with the question concerning the gracious God we are on another plane than that of the question concerning God. We are at the point where God asks: "Adam, where art thou?" (Gen. 3:9), "Saul, Saul, why persecutest thou me?" (Acts 9:4), "Whom seekest thou?" (John 18:4), and not where man asks: "Where is God?" To be sure, man does this too. He asks concerning the gracious God. But now, in this second event, the question has a very different quality. Its orientation is quite different. It is asked in dead earnest. The most suitable illustration for it is not the scrutinizing eye of man but the seeking, transfixing, demanding eye of God, which confronts us with ourselves and leads us to hell and back again.

One thing is clear. We cannot overhastily take refuge in our modern form of questioning or conclude too easily that we have substituted our more general question concerning God for Luther's question, as though the point at issue were now, not merely the grace of God, but the very magnitude of God. If we seek this kind of refuge, we entangle ourselves in hopeless complications with ourselves, from which the God of the Gospel seeks to free us. We may put it thus. As long as we take pleasure in our questioning, we take pleasure in our speaking and therefore in ourselves. And then we are not far from that delight in monologue which characterizes all secular religion.

If we are to have serious dealings with God it is essential that we be quiet and first of all do nothing but simply listen and let ourselves be questioned. When we do, we shall make the astonishing discovery that Christianity is not, as we supposed, an answer to our questions, and is therefore not a direct answer to the question "Where is God?" On the contrary, it is Christianity that asks the serious questions and therefore teaches us what true questioning is. Even the question concerning the gracious God is not a question with which we are to begin. It is rather the more advanced question of those whom God has already cured. We can see this surely from the story of the rich young ruler (Mark 10). He asks concerning eternal life, namely, concerning the possibility of finding eternal fellowship with God. But he receives no answer. Rather, Jesus Himself begins to ask questions. And He does so in such a way as to cause the question of the rich young ruler to recoil upon him. For He says, in effect, "You do not really want the kingdom of

God and in spite of your moral life and serious questions you
have no interest in fellowship with God. What you really
seek is yourself, though you are a little disturbed and excited
by the question of God, for if not, you would not be here,
rich man! What do you say? You have not sought yourself? You have sought God? You have kept the command-
ments, honoring your father and mother, loving your neighbors and thus submitting to God? Very well then, rich man,
sell all that you have, surrender yourself and let go of self.
Give an example of the fact that you do not belong to self
but to God. But you cannot do it. You will keep to self
and possessions; for you are only seeking self."

Thus the question concerning God recoiled upon the
rich young ruler the moment he himself was questioned by
God. It was made painfully clear to him that in spite of the
question concerning God, which he no doubt put with great
subjective seriousness, he was not really willing to be bound
to God and therefore to break free from self. It was made
clear to him that his final concern was not with God but
with himself. He thus arose sadly and went away unblessed.
He had expected an answer. He was faced only by a question.
He was too merciful to himself, this rich man. He would
not die to self. Hence God could not be merciful to him
and cause him to live. He then returned to his villa. And
perhaps he continued to toy with the question, "Where is
God?" He needed something like this question. And he
perhaps despised those of his acquaintances who asked concerning the gracious God. He perhaps accused them of
having fallen victims to the eyes of the Nazarene which he
himself had resisted. For apart from these eyes we do not get
to raise this question. He was quite right in this.

Caution is thus advisable in our judgments on the relevance
or irrelevance of the great questions of the Church. What
once was serious and no farce is still serious and no farce.
But the more serious it is, the less it is bandied about the
streets and the more humble and attentive and prayerful

we have to be to recognize it. So long as we have in our eyes the light of our human lamps, we do not see the eternal firmament but only our own immediate surroundings. To see it, we have to be in the dark and the human light must be gone from our eyes.

What we should do — and this is the will of God — is to refrain from testing the questions of the men of the Bible — the patriarchs, prophets and apostles — and of our own Reformers, from the standpoint of whether they are old-fashioned or modern, and to see them rather from the standpoint of whether we moderns have not perhaps forgotten and cast aside the realism which laid upon our forefathers such hard and troublesome questions. We are too prone to think that religious reality has changed. But perhaps it is simply we ourselves who have changed. Perhaps we have become more superficial and shallow and adept and slippery in maneuver — so shallow that our keel no longer detects the reef on which the little ship of our forefathers ran and was broken and wrecked. But the reef is still there.

We all realize what reef is meant, namely, the experience that we are not right with God; that we have no peace with Him and therefore no peace in our hearts; that our plight is not just that He is the infinite One and that we are but grains of dust and atoms (for no one is really caused to tremble by quantitative differences), but that we are enemies.

The peace of God, of which our forefathers knew something, does not consist, therefore, in drawing out this fact, but rather in the truth that in spite of everything God seeks us and that we may live in the power of His forgiveness.

Indeed, the question concerning the gracious God can now be given a different form. For instance, it may be formulated as follows: "How can I have fellowship with God in spite of all that there is between us?" Or, "How can I find my way out of unrest, doubt and despair to peace?" Or, finally, "How can I find my way out of security, out of the catastrophic absence of doubt and despair, to real peace?"

The formulation of the seeking after the gracious God depends on the situation in which we are placed. In an age of broken men who are visited by the preaching of a doctrine of Law, it may not sound at all the same as in an age — our age — of "secure" men — although we must make such generalizations with caution and allow for the obvious exceptions. The inner distress of a period may consist in undetected as well as in unsatisfied hunger. The latter case is that of the broken man, the former that of the secure. But the one distress is no less great than the other. "Surely all those who live so securely are but vanity" (Ps. 39).

Whatever form the question may take, however, it always arises out of the experience that we are not dealing with a "friendly" God, nor with a harmless Almighty, nor with an even more harmless Infinite, but that we have to do with the God who denies us because we deny Him, and who yet wants to be our Father. He does not pretend to be a merely friendly God; but He does want to be the forgiving Father. And at the point where this takes place there is no blanket to cover the dark background, the reef, of our plight, but there is the cross; there are the blood and tears of God. It costs Him something. For He loves us in truth and not innocuously. And this truth is the abyss. When God sets this reality before us and we see and face it, then we can put Luther's question concerning the gracious God in a new and different form, as we are able. We certainly do well to think it right through and not to rush by it too hastily. Yet however we then put it, we are not far from the kingdom of God.

7. Jesus' Conversation with Nicodemus by Night

> There was a man of the Pharisees, named Nicodemus, a ruler of the Jews:
>
> The same came to Jesus by night, and said unto him, Rabbi, we know that thou art a teacher come from God: for no man can do these miracles that thou doest, except God be with him.
>
> Jesus answered and said unto him, Verily, verily, I say unto thee, Except a man be born again, he cannot see the kingdom of God.
>
> Nicodemus saith unto him, How can a man be born when he is old? can he enter the second time into his mother's womb, and be born?
>
> Jesus answered, Verily, verily, I say unto thee, Except a man be born of water and the Spirit, he cannot enter into the kingdom of God.
>
> That which is born of the flesh is flesh; and that which is born of the Spirit is spirit.
>
> Marvel not that I said unto thee, Ye must be born again.
>
> The wind bloweth where it listeth, and thou hearest the sound thereof, but canst not tell whence it cometh, and whither it goeth: so is every one that is born of the Spirit.
>
> Nicodemus answered and said unto him, How can these things be?
>
> Jesus answered and said unto him, Art thou a master of Israel, and knowest not these things?
>
> Verily, verily, I say unto thee, We speak that we do know, and testify that we have seen; and ye receive not our witness . . . .
>
> For God so loved the world, that he gave his only begotten Son, that whosoever believeth in him should not perish, but have everlasting life (John 3:1-11, 16) .

IN THE NIGHT voices and noises come to life which we do not hear by day. When we walk through a dark wood by night, we hear very different and often more terrifying things than when the sun is shining through the branches. Even within ourselves there are voices by night which are not heard by day. Revolutions break out at night and are secretly plotted in darkness. Passions lift up their voices by night, whether in love or in hate. Lady Anxiety visits the camp by night and asks us the insistent and disturbing question, "How will things go tomorrow?" Conscience, which is dulled by day, takes on a new voice and appearance by night. The guilt of past days and nights stands up and begins to speak to us. And our pillow becomes a stone on which we can find no rest. It was such a night as this that Nicodemus came to Jesus.

For the questions concerning eternity also come to life at night. It was on a night when only the lamp burned and everything was quiet that Faust spoke of man's yearning for the streams of life, yes, for its very source.

By day things are quite clear to Nicodemus. He does his work, rules his family, does what is right, and is afraid of no one. This way life can to some degree be respectable and there cannot fail to be divine blessing. But then night comes, and in its shadow he is assailed by the question: Can the riddle of my life be solved so easily? Is there not something missing? I have no peace. My life rolls off into a void. What is this life all about? To be sure, I have made something of it. I have made my career. I have decorations. I have a gold chain of office. But does this constitute the meaning of my life? By day Nicodemus has no time for such reflections. He must write letters, receive callers, and do his business. But when darkness comes, it brings these thoughts with it. He knows that something is wanting. He cannot say precisely what it is, but he is conscious of the lack.

How is it that Nicodemus has an experience so very similar to our own? This night in which he comes to Jesus — can it really have been two thousand years ago? Does it not give expression to the night of our own lives? Do we not feel, too, that something is missing, that something decisive is missing, even though we cannot say precisely what it is?

60

Jesus' Conversation with Nicodemus by Night

Can we not find Nicodemus a hundred times over among us men whose lives are regulated by the clock and who are continually asking ourselves: What is the point of it all? Are we not circling around in a void? Can we not find him among industrialists and commercial leaders and those who have achieved success, but who are still asking where it all leads and whether their lives have really in the last analysis become different or richer? Can we not find him among technicians who wonder what will be the final end of their inventions and who perhaps ask with Diesel whether human life will really be prospered or made happier by them? Can we not find him among young mothers who ask how they are going to give to their children not merely the gift of life, but a life which is truly rich, which is filled with meaning, which will reflect eternity?

I ask again: Did this night really take place two thousand years ago?

Thus Nicodemus comes to Jesus, and all of us come with him. He has an obscure sense that Jesus has something to do with what I lack. Perhaps I will find peace there. Perhaps I will be able to fill the nameless, infinite void in my life. But he tries to play the role of the strong man. He does not lay his need before Jesus. He does not present his question. We are all too proud for that. There must be no show of weakness. An outward attitude must disguise the inner hollowness. Nicodemus comes only to discuss things with Jesus. He is not seeking pastoral help. And so he enters the room with a courteous greeting: "Rabbi, we know that thou art a teacher come from God: for no man can do these miracles that thou doest, except God be with him."

Will Jesus adopt the same polite conversational tone as His visitor? Does He see and hear that behind the mask of the official, of the technician, of the industrialist, of Nicodemus, lies the cry of a heart which has no peace?

But Nicodemus has already betrayed himself. For it is interesting to see whom and what he seeks in Jesus. He

seeks in Him neither the rising politician, nor the popular
Messianic leader, nor the great thinker and human teacher.
What has struck his attention is something very different,
namely, that Jesus performs miracles, that He can heal the
sick, that He comforts the despairing, that He even attacks
death and wrests from this bleak companion its victims,
that He, in general, has taken on the fight against all the
dark forces which disrupt our lives, that He breaks the
power of guilt, and . . . that He remains Victor in all
these things. This is what has struck the attention of
Nicodemus.

And this leads him to ask: Could not through this figure
fall a gleam of eternity into our lives which otherwise would
remain completely dark? Is there not manifest in Him something of the love of God, of His gracious visitation, of His
saving intervention in our lives, without which everything
seems so meaningless and dark and nonsensical? For is it
not madness that death can simply come and snap the bonds
of friendship and of love, that it can madly and blindly in-
trude into the world which we build without anyone calling
a halt to it? Is it not madness that men eat and drink and
marry and are given in marriage and that beyond this they
simply sleep and dream away the short time which after
all determines eternity? Is it not madness that guilt and the
principle of retribution should hold sway on the earth, that
evil acts should constantly give rise to fresh evil and that the
burdens of humanity should grow like an avalanche? Yet this
is what life looks like — or does it?

Who is to lift us out of this sea of madness? We are all
equally powerless at this point. No doctor, politician, or
economist can alter things. More clearly than ever we see
today that the destiny of the world has slipped out of the
hands of men and that it is not men who finally make history.

But here is One who is different from us. Here is One
before whom the powers of darkness yield. Here oppressed

bodies and tortured consciences are put right. All suffering steals away when the Saviour comes.

The Saviour! That is what Nicodemus is seeking. He is seeking One who is a match for suffering, anxiety and guilt. And he has this One in mind when he says: You do signs; you are different from us; you come from God. At root humanity is not looking for leaders or wise men, for these cannot help, because when one of our two legs is shot to pieces they have nothing to say.

Ultimately, men are not looking for outstanding "miracle men" (Luther), nor for politicians of genius who seem to make history. Such men may conquer other lands or raise the standard of living, but they are powerless to relieve my personal distress. They cannot alter the fact that I have a prodigal son, that my marriage has broken up, that I cannot control my dark thoughts. At these points they cannot help and I am all on my own.

Nor are men looking for doctors. Doctors are engaged in warfare with death, but they wage their battle in the shadow of death and will themselves finally succumb to it. What humanity, ourselves and Nicodemus included, is really looking for is the Saviour, who will be with each of us at every moment, who will heal our wounds and forgive our sins, who will enter the little boats of our lives and be with us no matter how high the waves, who will hide us in the hand of the Father. He is Himself this hand.

The truth is that at root very primitive things play the decisive role in our lives. Our stomach with its need of nourishment, our conscience with its lack of peace, and our death towards which we irresistibly move — these are the forces which decisively constitute life. The one who can master these, taking away anxiety, consoling the conscience and supporting us in dying, is the one for whom we truly look. Nicodemus had an obscure feeling that Jesus might be that person.

What does Jesus do when He sees the hungry and questioning look in the eyes of Nicodemus? He does something very matter-of-fact. It is night, and it is therefore easy to become emotional and religious. If the cheeks become red at the utterance of the word "God," this will not be seen.

But Jesus gives a most objective and, as it were, "non-religious" answer. "Verily, verily, I say unto thee, except a man be born again, he cannot see the kingdom of God." In these words Jesus is making what doctors call a diagnosis. He is listening and knocking on the inner heart of Nicodemus when He puts to him the question: "Are you born again?" For what does being born again mean?

Men born again are those who take seriously the fact that God is their Father. But to be children of the Father is to know that we are loved by Him and to reflect in our hearts the love received from Him, so that we also love our brothers. To be children of this Father is to dare to come back to Him as lost sons because His heart is waiting for us, and then to receive the power in turn to forgive our fellow men. To be children of this Father is to come to Him with all our cares and requests, saying, "Abba, dear Father." To be children of this Father is to trust in His love in hours of darkness and in difficulties, because a Father does not fool His children but always has for them the hidden thought of love.

The quiet words of Jesus go even further. It is not a matter of strained searching into the meaning of life or even into the mysteries of dogmas. A birth is not a matter of thought. It is a fact of life. God wants to come into your life, Nicodemus. Do you understand that? There is no sense in your trying to overcome the dead point of your life by further work, by trying to steel and stiffen your character, by mobilizing your inner reserves. If a man is on the wrong track, it is no use running faster. If you are not right within, your moral efforts are of no avail. Look, you must begin again at the very beginning. That is why I say that you must be born again. For birth is the first thing a man experiences.

Jesus thus lays bare the innermost heart of Nicodemus.

How will he react? Will he say: "Lord, you are right. Give me a new heart"? Will he cling to the Lord like a drowning man, and give himself to Him? No, he asks: "How can this be?" He is an old man. How can a person start all over again? How can he wipe out the past? How can he jump over his own shadow?

Instead of yielding to the Saviour, he seeks to enter into a highly intellectual conversation. He wants to discuss matters with Him. The question of how is the typical question of a man who wants to remain a spectator and not to come too close to the mystery that is Christ.

I have seen men who through preaching or through a disciple of Jesus have been touched and have suddenly seen the danger of being jolted out of their path by Jesus. I have noted how in such cases they often try to draw back. They prefer to do this by assuming the role of a partner in a discussion. They say: "Yes, the figure of Jesus is most impressive, most impressive. But how can there be a God-man? How can one who died be alive? How can one descend into hell?"

Those who think and speak thus are usually religious people who will not surrender. They profess sympathy with the Lord Jesus, but they refuse discipleship. They are interested, but they will not take up the cross. As soon as they are touched by Jesus, they assume the role of a questioner: How can this be?

Nicodemus is such a man. Jesus has attacked my heart, he thinks, but I have diverted the attack to the mind. That does not get so close to me, and that way we must first discuss things. The Nicodemus in us will not surrender to the Saviour. This is one of the reasons why he comes by night. No one must be able to say: "He also is with Jesus of Nazareth and has declared for Him." No one must see him with Jesus.

We wait anxiously to see whether Jesus will let Himself be drawn into this kind of debate.

No, that He will not. He does not answer the question. He simply repeats with great seriousness His saying concerning the new birth. It is as though He says: "I cannot and will not describe for you what the new birth is. It can only be experienced. And if it is not experienced, it cannot be understood. Then it is regarded as a rather queer inward disposition or something like that." But if it is experienced, if there is a surrender to Jesus and a yielding of the whole of life to Him, then there is no further question concerning the how.

To see this, we need only think of those who were healed by Him, such as the man born blind to whom He restored sight. Could this man describe and explain this encounter with Jesus to others? I do not think so. This is something which has to be experienced.

A person who in springtime must shout out his joy does not ask why. Similarly, there are many things in life which must be experienced to be known, and which otherwise cannot be explained, for example, love. If we have never loved, no one can ever describe to us what love is.

Hence Jesus cannot tell Nicodemus how this will be brought about. He can only say: "You must yield up your whole life to the Father in heaven, and then you will know." As Goethe tells us, we could never see the sun unless our eyes were sunny. And so we can never know who God is if we refuse to become "divine," to become children of God. This can be seen very easily from human relationships. Only a child can really know what motherly love is, or what is meant by a mother. Those who have had the misfortune not to know their mothers cannot learn from any description or from any psychological analysis what it is to have a mother.

This is the point Jesus makes in His conversation with Nicodemus: If you are not ready to become a child of the Father, then you will never know about the Father who loves you; then you will never know that I am your brother, that I will die for you. Then you will never know that you are the lost son, or how glorious is the Father's home whose doors are opened for you. You can never grasp these things, Nicodemus, unless you yourself become a child. Then there is also no point in our holding a solemn debate by night.

Do you not see, Nicodemus, that discipleship is not a matter of particularly learned thoughts or of a solemn discussion of the last things at night, but rather of the very sober question, Are you prepared, not just to talk about God, but to follow Him, and to do so wholeheartedly? I will not give you information about heavenly things, about life after death, about the mystery of grace, about the secret of My divine sonship, until you have grasped this fact and have become a child of God and have begun to put this into practice with your whole life.

Jesus Christ is known only in discipleship, or He is not known at all. All other talk about Him is only religious shadow-boxing, which leads to no results and in which the Lord refuses to take part, just as He refused to give information to Pontius Pilate because Pilate, too, did not ask with any readiness to hear or follow.

Truly, Nicodemus gets a rude awakening. There is no cozy talk about eternal things under the shining stars and in a solemn atmosphere. No, the world rocks under the feet of Nicodemus. He must be born again. His debating skill is powerless to extract himself neatly from this spot. When the eyes of Jesus are on us, we must keep still.

Yet Nicodemus asks again: "How can this be?" This time there is already a more serious ring to the question. Its temperature has suddenly changed. For what Nicodemus means is this: If, then, I am to become a child of God and to be born again, how is this to come about? A man cannot bear himself; he must be born. So there is nothing he himself can do about it. Everything depends, therefore, on God's doing something. But how can I make Him do anything in order that I may be a disciple, a child of God? Must

I wait passively for illumination, for the Holy Ghost to fall on me? How can these things be?

This time Jesus takes up the question, and at first it seems as though He is taking from Nicodemus any hope of being able to do anything.

The night wind is whistling around the house and rattling the windows. This suggests to the Lord a play on words, for in the original text the words "Spirit" and "wind" are the same. He says: "The wind bloweth where it listeth, and thou hearest the sound thereof, but canst not tell whence it cometh, and whither it goeth: so is every one that is born of the Spirit." This means that it all depends on our being touched by the Spirit of God. Only He can renew the heart. But one cannot give this Spirit to oneself. It is with Him as with the wind which we cannot control but which blows hither and thither and we cannot even determine its direction. Thus the final conclusion of wisdom seems to be that everything rests on the grace of God, on His sending the wind or Spirit.

But then we can clearly hear Nicodemus' inner outburst: How can this be? Perhaps it is grace, but do you not see that grace here is the utmost horror? Is it not terrible that the decisive point in my life (whether I shall obtain fellowship with God) should depend on something over which I have not the slightest influence? How, then, can I ever become a Christian?

Does not Nicodemus express here what troubles all of us? Jesus is the solution of our perplexities and problems, but we do not know how to cross the "broad and filthy ditch" of which Lessing spoke. Grace, grace — it sounds fine enough, but it is horrible and dreadful for those who do not know how to obtain it.

Nicodemus wraps himself in his cloak, for the night wind seems to have about it something as terrible and chilling as the grace of God. We cannot grasp the wind, nor can we grasp grace, but we need both of them to live. Without them we shall slowly choke, for life without union with God is like slow strangulation.

Jesus now says something quite remarkable, and in so doing He proves Himself to be a true pastor to Nicodemus: "We speak that we do know, and testify that we have seen." What He means is: Nicodemus, the Father is present in Me. You do not need to chase the wind. You have only to take My hand, and you will see that eternal life is bodily before you in Me; the divine breath touches you in Me.

Here the image of the stormy wind of God which blows where it wills all of a sudden takes on its comforting aspect. To be sure, we cannot make the wind blow. But we do not need to do so, for it is already blowing. Wherever the Son of God goes, the winds of God are blowing, the streams of living water are flowing, and the sun of God is smiling. He is the bodily guarantee that the sun and streams and wind of God are round me. I do not need to seek them. I am already encircled by the rush of wind and water and the radiance of light when Jesus begins to speak.

And He has indeed begun to speak. Are we not baptized? In this very hour He is in our midst. He has brought us here, and now He is present, quite simply present. We cannot make the storm of God; we have only to leap into it. Luther has expressed this triumphantly in his well-known saying: "A Christian is a man who leaps out of a dark house into the sun," and we read in our hymnbooks:

> *The sun which smiles upon me,*
> *Is my Lord Jesus Christ* . . . .

We ourselves cannot paint upon the heavens the rainbow of forgiveness that arches over our lives. We have only to place ourselves beneath it. But who is going to ask where it came from when it is simply there and inexplicably shines over us? Nicodemus, open the window. The winds of God are blowing outside, for your Saviour has come to you. Nicodemus, you man, you fool! You are wondering how to catch the sun of God into the net of your life. Do you not see, Nicodemus, that you are a simpleton for all your learning? Leap into the sun, Nicodemus, leap into the wind, for the sun shines and the wind of God roars; for Jesus Christ is standing before you!

8. Son of God or Brother Man

(To a Former Prisoner of War)

WHEN YOU THINK BACK to the days of your captivity and ask yourself how it really was that you held fast to Christ, you think that it must have been more than the "atmospheric" impression created by divine worship with its hymns and prayers, or the unsentimental mood of peace induced by the preaching of one of your comrades who was a chaplain.

You believe that you were impressed, not by a dogma — that Jesus Christ is the God-man — but by something very unecclesiastical. On the death of a comrade, your prison congregation sang: "When comes the day of parting, Do not depart from me. . . ." Then it struck you, and this impression was deepened by the sermon with its message, that the One to whom we thus cry is with us even in the last dark valley. What gripped you was the message that Jesus of Nazareth is our Companion, who suffers as we do, who is tempted as we are, who dies as we do, in order to be in all these things our Brother. And you add that He must have suffered hunger as we do, though you are not sure whether the Bible says so. And on Good Friday you heard His cry of dereliction on the cross: "My God, my God, why hast thou forsaken me?" and you knew that He was crying and suffering in exactly the same way as you and your companions. For the insistent question: Why? is with you day and night.

I also understand you very well when you write: "But when I heard that He, too, was afflicted by this torture of

dereliction, the dogmatic house of cards concerning the divine
sonship of Christ, which I had previously begun to build
around Him, suddenly collapsed. The marble facade of a
supposed divine sonship which had been erected around this
Jesus of Nazareth cracked. And for me there remained only
a poor and desperate man who suffered even to death by
reason of His overpowering task and even more so by reason
of the fact that He hung where He did because of an illusion.
I do not really know whether it was an illusion, and perhaps at that moment He himself did not know. He is supposed to have risen again, and then to have spoken very
differently. But this is alien to me, and means nothing to
me. But note well. If you think that I was sorry when
that house of cards of His divine humanity collapsed (forgive me, I do not mean to hurt you), and the hardly awakened
blossom of my new faith froze as in a night of spring frost,
you are much mistaken. Perhaps I lost what I had hardly yet
found — ecclesiastical faith. But I will not forget the comfort
and peace of the hour when I saw the man of Nazareth before me, not perhaps as He really was, but as He was de-
picted by the piety of those who loved Him and followed
Him in faith, namely, as a man who went out to be poor
with the poor, to be hungry with the hungry, to die with
the dying and to plunge Himself into wild and dreadful
forsakenness for the sake of those who in this fatherless world
cry out for a Father. For the only form of peace that He
was able to give was that all these people should know that
there is One who wants to be wholly ours. And even if
He cannot give them a Father, because there is none, He
will at least give them a Brother who bears this lack with
them and who plumbs their abyss of suffering to the very
depths. You see, that is the way He came to me. And even
if the myth of the Son of God broke up, in its place the
Brother of mankind gave Himself to me. He had indeed a
hand which can heal and comfort. He did not burden my
soul with a complicated dogma, but He stroked my forehead

as with a mother's hand. Because of this one moment I can never forget Him. Perhaps a minister will laugh sympathetically because I did not feel the breath of His Spirit (good Lord, what is this Spirit anyway?) but only the hem of His garment, a sorry piece of cloth. You see, I am only a poor proletarian of the Christian world and only stand like an onlooker before a lighted window behind which you sit with your friends at a royal table. But do not forget him who sees the light, even though he is not seen by it."

Dear friend, if you count me among those who may sit within, let me tell you how very concerned we should be not to deprive you of the promise which certainly applies to those like you, namely, that the messengers of the king are to go to those in the highways and the hedges, to those who stand afar off and dare not lift up their heads, to those who hunger and thirst after righteousness. When you say all these things as you do in your letter, we church Christians sense among us the ugly demon of security and comfortable possession; then we see not only the blessing but also the curse of assured traditions, and we wish we were again among those afar off to whom the promise applies. The peace of God is not something we can rest on, but for which we must reach. And we possess the Lord Christ only to the extent that we have the word of His Father: "Ye may be my children," and thus cherish the sacred hope that He will not despise a troubled spirit and a contrite heart.

If I thus call down to you from the lighted window — we will stick to your comparison, and let us hope that it is not a Pharisee who is looking out — I do not do this like a plutocrat calling to a proletarian, but like one who himself has only just been called in and who knows that he may continually enter afresh even though he, too, is out there in the dark by the hedge.

And please do not think that I am now going to say that you have an imperfect picture of the Lord in your heart. Do not think that I am anxious to build up again as quickly as possible what you call the dogmatic house of cards. You are quite right in suspecting that I regard it as something more and different than a house of cards. But perhaps this had to happen to you, perhaps the house of cards had to collapse, because the divine sonship of the Lord was for you not a mature confession or experienced truth, but indeed a house of cards. It is true even of the holy house of this dogma that it must be founded upon the rock if it is to stand. But in your case it was founded only upon the shifting sand of concepts, and this sand has caused the house to crack. It has, moreover, clogged up your thinking mechanism, for which sand is no more helpful than for other machines.

You are perhaps surprised that I surrender this dogma so lightly. Rest assured, however, that I am not really doing so. I am simply approaching you from another angle, and I am confident that you will stumble upon it again at a later date.

In the Gospels we are constantly told of people who, when they meet Jesus, suddenly realize who He is. They then exclaim: "You are the Christ, you are the Son of God." It is not necessarily only disciples who do this. Even those who are possessed, even unclean spirits, do.

Now one might reasonably expect that Jesus would be pleased at this recognition, and that He would appreciate having it proclaimed among the people and made widely known. Strangely enough, the very opposite is true. He charged these people to keep silent. The liberating word concerning His person and mission — the word which could enter with revolutionary and creative force into untold lives — is sealed with the seal of secrecy. How are we to understand this? Scholars refer to it as the Messianic secret.

I must explain this to you since it might well throw a whole new light on your own situation. Tradition had attached to the Messianic title, and therefore to the title "Son of God," a fixed meaning, and invested it with a very definite content. You know from schooldays how the Jews were looking for an earthly ruler who would deliver Israel from its external enemies (Luke 24:11). The danger therefore existed that Jesus of Nazareth would be linked with these traditional beliefs that were stirring in the popular imagination. In that event, the people would be prejudiced and measure Him by standards imported from without. And if He did not measure up to them — and the Crucified of Golgotha certainly did not — then He would be rejected and regarded as a fraud from the standpoint of this exaggerated idea. It could hardly be otherwise.

Today we understand better why Jesus sealed men's lips and demanded secrecy. He did not want to be forced into a ready-made dogma and thus be misunderstood, nor did He want to enforce recognition by suggesting a lofty title and profiting from it. Many might address Him with such a title and yet be quite untouched by Him in their hearts. They might be content to have it in black and white — "He is the Messiah" — and then to go home satisfied in the less satisfactory sense of the term.

Do you notice something? Perhaps in your case God has shattered the house of cards for similar reasons. Perhaps He did not want you to look on the Lord from the standpoint of this traditional and often terribly distorted, dissected and abstract concept of divine sonship. Perhaps it is a breath from God which has blown down your house of cards. And I admit that in many conversations with young seekers after God I have learned to conceal the Messianic title, and I do so just because I am so overwhelmingly conscious that Jesus of Nazareth alone bears it, and that He is "my Lord and my God."

Jesus did not conceal this title because He did not accept it, but because He did not want men to misuse it. He wanted men to encounter Himself and to learn for themselves to see in Him the reflection of the Father's heart. He wanted them to see how He forgave sins and healed the sick and raised the dead. And then He expected them at the very last to

say: "Thou are the Christ, the Son of the living God," and
to say this with a knowledge which could only express itself
thus, which indeed was compelled to do so. Jesus did not
desire confession of His divine sonship to be a presupposition
of meeting Him. He desired it rather to be the result of
such a meeting when it had taken place.

Surely you now understand why the man Jesus of Nazareth, who is all that is left to you, why this brotherly Man
who enters into all your troubles, is not the tragic remnant
of a shattered doctrine of Christ. Rather, surely you understand why now all the promises must apply to you since you
have really begun to see Him.

Therefore you need do no more than try to know Him
better as a man, as a mere man. Read the Gospels as ac-
counts of a noble and brotherly man. Even go so far as to
take from the sermons which you hear only that which con-
tains, or seems to contain, statements concerning this man,
this man of destiny for you. And since you have psychological interests, you may even measure Him by these standards
to know His inner life. For the moment, I tell you only this.
Along these lines you will one day work up from below
to above until you reach a point where your scheme will
break down and your human estimation will no longer be
adequate. And in this moment you may be sure that you
are drawing near to Him as He truly is.

We cannot draw God too deeply into the flesh, as Luther
once said. For this reason there is great promise if you begin
with the flesh until it suddenly dawns on you who is really
encountering you in this flesh. And this will be a more
genuine encounter than if you begin with lofty concepts.
"The Word became flesh," we read in the Gospel. But we
never read: "God became a concept." Concepts are made
only by theologians. I myself am a theologian. I am so
by conviction and, I believe, by commission. I would not be
anything else. But for this very reason I know the position
occupied by concepts in relation to reality. I also know

that we cannot do without them. But if we begin with them, we build a house of cards and one day the storm will come and blow it away. If we conclude with them, they can then be the facade of a real house and can thus contain the praise with which we honour the Most High in our thinking too.

Take very seriously, then, the human and brotherly features which have struck you in Jesus of Nazareth. And now I will return to your metaphor of the hem of the garment. Cling firm to this hem. Perhaps for the moment this is all that you have in your hands. There was another one who touched the hem of His garment (Matt. 9:20). It was a poor, sick woman who came up behind Him and was too shy to look Him in the face. Others might boast that they had shaken His hand, or had looked Him in the eye, or had spoken with Him. She could only be silent and ashamed, for she had simply touched the hem of His garment. But how many of those who perhaps said then, "This is the Messiah, the Son of God," and saw Him face to face, later fell away from Him and died without His consolation! Yet this woman, who only touched the hem of His garment, came to see His glory and was cured that very moment.

Those who have the hem of His garment in their hands have the promise that they have the whole Saviour. You now hold it in your hands. Be sure to hold it fast. To be sure, it is only the garment, not the hand or the heart. But it is the garment of the Saviour. He is willing to be held by this garment of His humanity. One day He will turn round and face you. There is no doubt about that. He will ignore the crowd of inquisitive or indifferent spectators thronging Him. He will address Himself directly to you. He will ask, "Who are you, that you touch Me? Virtue has gone out of Me."

Therefore hold on to what you have, even though it is only this poor hem. You have the promise that one day it will be a crown.

9. *World History and World Judgment*

(1948)

JOSEPH WITTIG ONCE SAID that a biography should not begin with the birth of the person but rather with his death. It should be written in the light of the end, for only from this point can we see a life in its fullness. If we think of history, or at any rate the writing of history, as a kind of biography of the world, a similar thesis might be advanced.

Before we examine how far this thesis can be illustrated on a Christian view of history, it is perhaps well for us to realize that the application of the thesis to history is made possible only by certain considerations as to the inner course of historical development. Thus, if we isolate small sectors of history or specific phases in a person's life, it is difficult to perceive any dominant meaning. This is why we often read of momentary successes. The expression is designed to indicate that success at one point does not really tell us whether a work or venture or battle deserves to last or will last, and therefore whether there is any significant connection between achievement and reward. A single moment does not show us whether a worthy act receives its reward or an evil one avenges itself. The system on the basis of which there is reward or retribution, or, theologically, the higher will which apportions reward or punishment, can be seen, if at all, only in wider fields and over longer periods. The moment is ruled by chance. Chance is a category of the moment. Chance as we are now using it is not a statement as to content. It does not mean that there is no choice or that we are engaged in a hopeless journey into the void. It is a statement as to one aspect from which I can view events, the aspect of the moment.

The author of Psalm 73 considers the momentary successes of the rich and the powerful and the ungodly, who assert themselves and who always seem to succeed (as contrasted with the righteous and in apparent defiance of all justice), until we consider their end, that is, until we extend our view to the totality of their lives: "I went into the sanctuary of God; then understood I their end." Here the aspect of chance is altered in two ways.

First, the Psalmist transcends the moment by considering the totality of life, by turning, as it were, to the final frontier of the lives of these knights of fortune. Secondly, he transcends the moment by going into the sanctuary and therefore by viewing the successes of the moment from the standpoint of eternity. In both cases he stands at a distance and considers the boundaries. In the light of the boundaries he sees the law which binds together the chance moments into a continuous chain. One of the laws which is disclosed is that of guilt and retribution. This law is very largely hidden. Theologically, we are forced to say that even where it seems to be disclosed it is still always hidden in its true and proper sense. Nevertheless, it must also be said that certain contours of an order of guilt and retribution can be traced. In this sense Bismarck once said that the reckonings of history are more exact than the audits of the Prussian treasury.

It is important to consider this. For since the collapse of 1945 our German contemplation of history has been particularly concerned with this law of longer periods. With its help attempts have been made to attribute the collapse not to the fate of the moment — for example, the exhaustion of armaments potential, or biological reserves, or tardiness in the invention of the atom bomb — but rather to the law of guilt and retribution. It is rightly recognized that to do this we must go back in history a long way. There is thus a tendency to make not only Bismarck but already Frederick the Great and even the Reformation responsible for false developments which have only reached their culminating point in our own decade. The illusion of a total view is created by turning constantly further back. This does not, however, give us history in its totality. All that results is a form of historiography which might be called history-writing on the basis of criminology. The field of historical study is full of busy detectives trying to track down the original source of mischief on the view that the true criminals in the foreground, including those condemned at Nuremberg, seem to be the victims or agents of an evil spirit of the age which was corrupted long ago. In this concern of criminal history to trace the head of these great conspiracies and thereby to extend constantly the radius of historical action, there is a correct, if rather distorted, realization that when we think in terms of guilt and retribution we must press to the very horizon of history. The full law is seen only at the boundary. But where is the boundary of history?

At this point we might recall a parallel from physics, namely, the law of averages. If we restrict ourselves to a narrow field, for instance, to a single electron, chance seems to rule. But statistics concerns itself with averages, and here the irrationality of detailed individual events is incorporated into a larger regularity. The same is obvious in history. What seems in detail to rest on imponderable freedom — for instance, suicide — proves to be a constant and regular magnitude when investigated on its average through whole countries or continents. Now obviously in history, too, we have to go by averages if we are to arrive at law, namely, the law that in the long run certain things will be avenged and others rewarded.

The whole field of vision must be before us if we are to fix this law exactly. But the claim to have this whole field before us is identical with the claim to know the boundary of history, or, more strictly, to occupy a place of transcendence.

Any illegitimate attempt to wrest this position from within history itself, however, is avenged by the fact that ultimately such an attempt does not lead to understanding but to its very opposite, namely, to blindness. For hardly is the law of guilt and retribution disclosed by one segment of the field before it is again even more concealed the very next moment. For what results from a bird's-eye view, from the greatest possible field of vision, which after all can never be more than that of a mere observer, is not really the law of guilt and retribution, but fate or blind necessity.

This may be seen from the morphology of history advanced by Oswald Spengler, within which there is no place for moral and religious categories like those of guilt and destiny. According to this cultural morphology, history is finally interpreted only in analogy to nature. This naturalizing and de-moralizing of history is finally betrayed by the single fact that Spengler understands the thousand-year course of civilizations in terms of the natural rhythm of epochs and therefore of something quite empty of moral values. This means that there is no place for freedom and responsibility, within which guilt and judgment are possible. A law seems to be perceived, but at once its inward substance is altered. It is no longer a law of history; it is a law of nature.

What we observe here is not merely to be noted empirically. It gives evidence of a theological process. The bird's-eye view arose from the necessity to attain to a maximum field of vision. But the whole field can be seen only from the boundary, from a transcendent vantage-point, and therefore from a distance. For this reason the bird's-eye view is, theologically, a usurped transcendence. It is the attempt to lift oneself above history in order to survey it and to cross its boundary from within. But it has the same result as all such transgressions — one's view is obscured rather than enlightened. Our first forefathers, who crossed the boundary to God that they might become as God, did not in fact become as God but forfeited their filial relationship and were expelled from Paradise. Therefore, whatever the truth of Goethe's saying that those who act are always right, there can be no doubt that those who *observe,* that is, who cross the boundary and take a bird's-eye view, are always wrong.

For the construction of a Christian concept of history it is absolutely vital that the transcendence necessary for the perception of guilt and retribution should not be won from within history but that transcendence should break into history from without and then occur within it. This presence of transcendence in history is Jesus Christ. In Him the provision is met that one can speak of sin and retribution, and therefore of judgment too, only in the light of the whole and from the standpoint of the end. He has not unjustly been called the center of history. This idea is of great symbolical force for our consideration of the totality of history, for we can understand the center here as the elevated middle point from which the horizon of history can be scanned both backwards and forwards. In fact, the New Testament gives expression to this fact, and therefore to the aspect of history, in many different ways.

From the standpoint of Christ the horizon of history is revealed backwards when it is said that the world was created by Jesus Christ. This obviously implies that in Him it is evident that from the very first the history of the world has been oriented to salvation. To adapt another saying of Goethe, one might almost say that the secret of history is not so much the conflict between faith and unbelief as between salvation and perdition. History is the sphere in which one is summoned to come back from afar to fellowship with God. This alone is the secret of the many individuals, often anonymous, who are nevertheless known to God. This alone is the destiny of kings and dictators and great historical figures with their realms, who all, as Blumhardt once said, stand under the sign of going whereas the kingdom of God stands under the sign of coming. History is aimed from the very first at something which Christ represents from the very first, namely, salvation.

From the perspective of Christ as center, history is also revealed forwards. Christ will come again to judge the quick and the dead. He will wind up history. Negatively, this means that the winding up does not form part of the continuity of history. The real end of adventurers and ruffians is not manifested within history. But at the end of history, when the harvest will be reaped, when all things will be terminated and when the great grave of the world will yawn, everything will be plain, for at this frontier stands the King with His sickle and His crown, who knows what is in man and who has not lost sight of this secret of man — of every man.

At the center itself, however, and not merely on the horizon, there is also manifested the judgment of history. For if here there is a resurrection from the dead on the third day, then death is not understood as a biological law and hence a morally indifferent event. It is seen to be an unnatural thing, a hostility, a rent in creation. As here the sick are healed and the suffering comforted, we see the unsaved world waiting for the great day of redemption. As here sins are forgiven and remission is pronounced with authority as an inbreaking miracle, there is manifestation of hopeless bondage to the entail of guilt and to ineluctable law.

Here it is true — though in a terribly different way — that world history is world judgment. I ask you to take this now quite literally. World history does not merely bring judgments and retributions in the form of individual events, that is to say, along the lines of what the aged harper in Goethe's *Wilhelm Meister* says: "All guilt is avenged on earth," for often this is not true. No, history is itself the judgment. It is under judgment. *In toto* it is riveted to what cannot be altered, namely, to the fact that since the mysterious separation known as the fall man must henceforth be guilty, that there can be no escape from what Frank Thiess calls the "torture chamber of history," that we are all implicated in the terrible process of war and warlike clamor, where it is unalterably fixed that "some are in darkness and some are in light," that all men are guilty and that all men must die.

Yet we have not really told the whole story concerning the relation between history and judgment if we stop at this general aspect of the nexus. We must probe deeper and ask whether in this light the question does not arise in a new and different form, whether we cannot describe specific events — for example, the German disaster — as judgment.

If there is a Christological center of history, and if the secret of history rests in a figure who is not to be encompassed intellectually but who goes about *incognito* and can be grasped only in the venture of faith, then our first point must be that the judgment is not a simple object of vision but an object of faith. I can speak of judgment only if I know the Judge, the Person who decides. Here the analogy to our human judicial processes breaks down. In these processes the important thing is not to know the judge but the laws by which he judges and of which he is an officer. God, however, is not the officer of an order superior to Him. He establishes all order by His sovereign will alone. In exactly the same way as I cannot argue from creation to the Creator, as though everything corruptible were a true and perspicuous simile, but can read the secret of creation only if I know the Creator and His heart, so I perceive the secret of judgments only if I know the One who judges. A first implication of this is, of course, that judgment is invisible in just the same way as the Judge and the things of faith generally are invisible.

We shall now try briefly to elucidate this hiddenness of judgment that is manifested only through the person of the Judge. That one cannot objectively make assertion of judgment is obvious even on the secular level from the fact that such assertion is ambiguous in principle. The song sings of the shattered armies of Napoleon in Russia: "With wagons, men and horses, Has God dispersed their forces." But do we really have here an unequivocal judgment of God on Napoleon? Perhaps a Frenchman might not unjustly reply that, if we are to speak of judgment and not simply to apply the category of the tragic, Europe rather than Napoleon was the power smitten by God, since Europe lost in this way the Napoleonic principle of order and its blessings. Europe had the chance, he might argue, to come under the living influence of a great political conception, and with the fall of Napoleon it sank back into the decadence of its own outworn tradition. Napoleon, then, was rather the executor of this judgment on Europe. The metaphysical role as well as the character of the great figures of history is thus difficult to fix with precision. And therefore is not every pronouncement of judgment relativized?

Even in regard to more obvious disasters, which perhaps impose sacrifice far less equivocally than the Napoleonic events (e.g., the German disasters of 1918 and 1945, or life-long sickness), the diagnosis "divine judgment" always comes up against a final limit at which we are forced to inquire anew: Can this suffering be deduced causally from some preceding guilt? Does it not admit of a non-final explanation, one, for instance, in terms of a divine purpose of instruction? Are not these two interpretations mutually exclusive to the degree that in the one disaster and suffering have the character of wrath (judgment) and in the other of salvation (instruction)? In the story of the man born blind (John 9, especially 1-3), the two interpretations clash very dramatically in the conversation between Jesus and the disciples. The disciples build on the self-evident assumption that some guilt must be responsible for the fate of blindness from birth, that it therefore bears the character of judgment. Jesus, however, turns the causal explanation of the disciples into what seems to be the completely different teleology, that this blindness serves the purpose "that the works of God should be made manifest in him."

In this case, too, we again seem to be confronted by an insoluble ambiguity. For who would dare to interpret the situation so fully along the lines asserted by Jesus and therefore to wrest from it a disclosure of the unequivocal divine message? It is surely conceivable — we shall have to follow this up more closely — that the concrete message of judgment is not discredited by the ambiguity, but that there lies behind it a true and valid question concerning what then the judgment of God is and whether what seems to us to be ambiguity may not perhaps express very plainly the fact that we are dealing with two complementary constituents of judgment, judgment being both punishment for the past and instruction for the future, both rejection and visitation, both condemnation and salvation.

This reflection, however, leads us back to the decisive point, that the secret of judgment, whether as retribution for the past or visitation for the future, is disclosed only in the light of the person of the Judge, which means only in the light of faith.

There is another theological reason why objective assertion of judgment is impossible. This is the fact that the judgments of God might consist in His silence. The fact that no correspondence can be asserted between guilt and punishment because God is sometimes silent and passive when according to our ideas He ought to come down in a storm of judgment and make clear examples, usually involves us in severe struggles and temptations and brings us under the full force of the problem of theodicy. Yet it is not true that God is doing nothing when He seems to be silent and passive. Judgment may then be exercised; indeed, it may consist in this very silence and passivity. In the language of faith this means two things. First, it means that God withdraws His arm and abandons men to themselves, thus giving them up to the results of their own actions and delivering them to self-judgment. The very moments when the ungodly feel secure because God is silent, and when they mock the divine judgments because they confuse the terrible act of divine withdrawal with the non-existence of God, are the moments when faith may see the judgments of God lying with particularly crushing weight on the world, so that the outbreak of an open storm of wrath is felt to be a relief from the sinister oppressiveness of silent judgment.

We thus see that even God's silence in relation to the world, even the apparent non-fulfillment of judgment, is not to be understood as though we men had no "antennae" by which to detect the relationship, or as though the impression that God is silent were the result of our deaf ears and hardened hearts, or as though, in other words, the silence of the Judge were connected merely with the unreceptivity of our own subjective structure.

No, the silence of the Judge is an objective phenomenon. It is part of the manner of divine judgments. Even the angels around the throne of God can bear witness to the reality of God's silence. It does not rest on impressions that are due to human obduracy. God can really be silent. He does not judge only or even perhaps primarily by bringing down on the transgressors lightning strokes or other disasters *ex machina*. He also judges by silent abstention. This is how He judged the builders of the tower of Babel for their ungodliness. By doing nothing, He caused them to fall into confusion and dispersion in their ungodliness. Thus His silence was supreme activity. What He allowed to happen took on the form of collapse and confusion. God was powerfully at work in their confusion simply by looking on. In the same way He abandoned the heathen to their own state (Romans 1:18ff.).

This handing over (*paredoken*) is the mode of silent judgment, although at first glance it might seem that no more is evident here than the law of sin and retribution.

Let us try to bring out the open and the hidden aspects of this judgment in terms of Romans 1:18ff. Here perversion on the horizontal plane corresponds to disorder on the vertical, namely, self-assertion before God. But if the result seems to be plainly one of self-avenging or of vengeance, there is also a measure of concealment. The perverts of Romans 1 would probably have been most astonished at any references to their supposed plight. They undoubtedly had an individual sense of security.

The same was probably true of those who built the tower of Babel. They probably argued that war and conflict, that the power of destruction and strife, that all the things in and by which we are torn out of our original state of peace, of being of one speech and language, are in fact "the father of all things," the basic impulse of life. They may well have believed that a measure of ungodliness, of Satanism, serves to keep the world alive:

> *A man is prone to slacken his ambition,*
> *For rest and peace is what he likes and craves.*
> *That's why I like to give him for companion*
> *A man who like the devil toils and slaves.*

This, then, is the concealment of judgment, that man thinks the final extremity of a deranged world is a virtue.

All that we have previously affirmed concerning the way in which the divine judgment is manifested was simply an exposition of the truth that the secret of judgment can be known only in the light of the Judge. As long as we do not know the personal "Thou" of the Judge, who, paradoxically, also appears as our Father in Jesus Christ, we are hopelessly at sea in relation to the question how the world-order functions and with what efficiency. We use the word "hopelessly" in the strict sense, not only because the torturing question of why can never be stilled, but also because it can never be solved, because it remains insoluble.

The chief and representative forms of this insolubility take two main directions: either the question leads us to the final assertion of inscrutability, that is to say, that there is no way out, whereby the next step is the nihilistic insight that there is nothing to scrutinize, that the world is without either

Ruler or Father; or it leads us to the statistical perspective of averages, and therefore to an assertion of the frigid regularity and silence of nature. A combination of the first and second answers is to be found in the attempt to interpret the finite world tragically, that is to say, to assert an order which neither gods nor men can question, which is ineluctable fate, and concerning which we know neither by whom it was ordered nor to what end. This situation, in which man no longer understands judgment because he has lost the Judge, is itself a judgment.

The solution which the biblical message brings to this hopeless problem of meaning, to this painful secret of history with its hidden judgments, does not consist in an answer to the question of why but in changing the question: To what end? I turn again to the story of the man born blind. The disciples ask why he was born blind. Who sinned? Jesus, however, asks to what end he bears this affliction, and He answers: "That the glory of God should be made manifest in him."

The question concerning why has a causal orientation, and it demands the answer: "Because God did this or that." But such an answer cannot be given. It is concealed in a higher counsel.

The question to what end does not demand this kind of answer; rather, it is satisfied with the certainty that we may let ourselves be surprised because we are protected, because there is no Midgard serpent on the horizon, because the world has a Fatherly basis. This is why the Christian does not say, "Because . . ." in face of the riddle of history; he says rather: "Yet I am still with Thee." For he sees judgment in the light of the Judge, who is none other than the Father upon whom we may call and whose children we may assuredly be in Jesus Christ.